THE INTERPRETATION OF PIANO MUSIC •

Publisher's Note

The book descriptions we ask book-sellers to display prominently warn that this is an historic book with numerous typos or missing text; it is not indexed or illustrated.

The book was created using optical character recognition software. The software is 99 percent accurate if the book is in good condition. However, we do understand that even one percent can be an annoying number of typos! And sometimes all or part of a page may be missing from our copy of the book. Or the paper may be so discolored from age that it is difficult to read. We apologize and gratefully acknowledge Google's assistance.

After we re-typeset and design a book, the page numbers change so the old index and table of contents no longer work. Therefore, we often re-move them; otherwise, please ignore them.

Our books sell so few copies that you would have to pay hundreds of dollars to cover the cost of our proof reading and fixing the typos, missing text and index. Instead we let most customers download a free copy of the original ty-po-free scanned book. Simply enter the barcode number from the back cover of the paperback in the Free Book form at www.RareBooksClub.com. You may also qualify for a free trial membership in our book club to download up to four books for free. Simply enter the barcode number from the back cover onto the membership form on our home page. The book club entitles you to select from more than a million books at no additional charge. Simply enter the title or subject onto the search form to find the books.

If you have any questions, could you please be so kind as to consult our Fre-quently Asked Questions page at www. RareBooksClub.com/faqs.cfm? You are also welcome to contact us there. General Books LLC™, Memphis, USA, 2012.

⊰⊱ ⊰⊱ ⊰⊱ ⊰⊱ ⊰⊱ ⊰⊱ ⊰⊱ ⊰

I c

The Interpretation of Piano Music TO MY MOTHER PREFACE

A German authority has remarked that if it were as easy to read music as to read words, "the sonatas of Beethoven would have the popularity of the poems of Schiller." The difficulty of compre-hending the full import of music written for the pianoforte arises from the fact that the signs representing the concep-tions of the composer are variable and inaccurate, being, at best, suggestive, but never absolutely precise.

The prime object of the work here of-fered to the student is to assist him in acquiring a correct understanding of the visible language of music; to gather the significance of the abbreviated modes of a notation which must be rightly in-terpreted by the mind before the music can be conveyed to the ear by means of the mechanism of the pianoforte. Very little attention has been given to the sub-ject in printed publications, and these pages are intended to set forth the prin-ciples involved, in a way that is not merely of theoretical interest but is also of practical value.

It is believed that this brief treatise is the first which adequately considers the matters brought to the reader's attention under the topics: Bowing-signs, Musi-cal Symbols and their Meaning; How to Find a Hidden Melody; Harmony: Du-ration and Dynamics of Tones in the Different Voices; A Theme of Chopin Interpreted; and Orchestration at the Pianoforte. Some portions of the discus-sion of the Appoggiatura and the Ac-ciaccatura will be found at variance with the explanations often given of these terms, which aye sometimes con-fused even by high authorities. The chapter on The Pedals, the substance of which was first presented in the form of lectures, considers the topic with spe-cial reference to Notation, lays stress on the necessary cooperation of the fin-gers with the feet, gives a bibliography

and ls of pedal notation formerly in common use.

From time to time, since July, 1902, much of the matter of this volume has appeared in *The Musician,* Boston, *The Etude,* Philadelphia, and *The Courier,* Cincinnati; but every paragraph has been carefully revised, and in many in-stances the original papers have been considerably amplified.

The author wishes to acknowledge deep indebtedness to her honored mas-ter, Signor Albino Gorno, for many facts here embodied. —

Mary Venable. CONTENTS

The Interpretation Of Piano Music CHAPTER I

The Language Of Music

The art of reading a piece of litera-ture, an essay, for example, or a poem, consists of gathering into the mind from the printed page the meaning contained in and Reading suggested by the words and sentences which deflned constitute the particular work perused. If the read-er possess the knowledge requisite to a complete understanding of all the words, sentences and punctuation marks in their separate values and in their logical and grammatical relations, he may fully comprehend and appreciate the essay or the poem, possibly at a single reading, having, through the eye, taken into his consciousness the impressions which the author intended to convey by means of the arbitrary forms at his command. Subjectively, such a reader has mastered the content of thought and of feeling represented by the text which visually and mentally he has inspected. Should he desire to communicate to another the impression he has received from the printed page, he may, by the organs of speech, render audible and intelligible the significance of the same piece of literature. In the necessarily more or less mechanical process of embodying the silent spirit of the composition in vocal utterance he will be much aided by the devices invented for facilitating spoken speech, namely, articulation, accent, emphasis, tone-qualities, pauses, — in a word, elocution. On the inspired lips of a, genius like Novelli or Edwin Booth, even the best language of a supreme dramatist receives a new and incalculable value of interpretative art.

There is a close analogy between the method of learning to read a piece of literature, especially a poem, and that of learning to read a piece of music, for there may be said to be a language of music,though to the eye it differs essentially Music and from ordinary written or printed language. The rhythmic thoughts, concepts or emotions which it is the speech function of the composer of music to convey to the mind, through either the eye or the ear, or through both, are not represented by words of definite, limited meaning, arranged in the usual grammatical and logical sequence, but they are represented by other sets of symbols which, like words, are recognizable to the eye by their form and to the ear by their sound. The purpose of musical expression is certainly no less exact than that of poetical expression, and the written language of music, slowly developed through the centuries, has become an exceedingly complex and intricate system, often very difficult to master. Nevertheless it is evident that until the student has ac-

quired skill in the ready understanding of what confronts him on the puzzling pages of his musical score, — until, as Berlioz says, "he divines music before he has read it," — he cannot hope to take silent pleasure from reading it to himself, much less give pleasure by translating it into the vibrations of a singing voice or of the strings of a piano. The artist, whether vocal or instrumental, must somehow get the music into his soul before he can bring it to his tongue and lips or to the tips of his fingers. Therefore the first necessity for the student of music is, Learn to read! And the second? Learn to read! And the third? Learn to read!

It is fundamental to any symbolized scheme of music that there should be at least a staff, a clef and some notes. To Music a these essentials have been added numerous ac symboiized cessory marks and devices, such as the slur, the language dot, the bar, the rest, to aid the reader to an easier and more felicitous understanding and interpretation of the elementary mechanism just mentioned.

The notes, which singly and in combinations of varying complexity constitute the main body of the text of a piece of music, represent tones, and they may be said to correspond to the letters, especially the vowels, of ordinary language, which represent elementary sounds. The smallest organic unit in music is not the note or tone, but consists of a group of notes or tones. Such a group, having a certain com-The period pleteness or pleasing effect in itself, though never the phrase and independent of its organic relations to the whole Itssu composition of which it is a vital part, is recognized by musicians as a *motive,* and forms an integral member of a phrase. The phrase, though bearing a resemblance to the phrase of the grammarian, cannot be identified with that, but is peculiar to the art of music. Indeed, what is known as phrasing is one of the complicated and difficult subjects of musical study. The process of musical phrasing, or resolving the composition into intelligible and component ideas, is comparable to the grammatical analysis of complex sentences in ordi-

nary language. When we consider that the phrase is "the structural basis of all musical forms," we realize how important an element in musical education is that which consists in teaching pupils to discern with accuracy just what is included in each successive phrase and just how the phrase as a whole is related to its subordinate parts and to other complete phrases. Much confusion prevails even in the writings of authorities of good reputation in regard to the precise meaning of the words "phrase" and "phrasing," and a reckless terminology, confounding the application of such names as half-phrase, section, motive, phraselet and figure, and these with the phrase of which they are but subdivisions or members, befogs the mind and misleads the practice of earnest learners of music. The true musical phrase, owing to its integral character and relative independence, corresponds somewhat to the simple sentence of ordinary language; but it is to be observed that, in music, also, the terms "sentence" and "period" are specially employed to designate a melody extending through a series of measures and having a certain completeness larger than that of the phrase, and comprising in itself two phrases and sometimes more than two. Sentential subdivisions may begin at any part of a measure, whether it be unaccented or accented. The musical period or sentence corresponds, in some degree, to the stanza of poetry; and, indeed, the province of the composer of music and that of the builder of "lofty rhyme" lie very near together and, in some cases, appear to overlap each other.

Musical articulation may be defined as the act of forming, in song, or by means of instruments, or by combinations of any Purposes of of tnese the elements of musical language. The musical articulate character of music depends upon a articulation division of collocated tones with reference to component single tones and the uniting of these together into intelligible groups so as to form so-called motives. Each tone should have its due proportion of sound so that the ear shall easily perceive either its detachment from other tones or its connection with other tones. In music, as in oral speech, a good articulation gives greater power and reach than the loudest vociferation can give. The objects of musical articulation are to show the derivation or composition of figures, motives and passages and to divide musical groups properly when disconnection is desirable. By false division of the tones these objects are defeated, the text is misrepresented, and the music is rendered unintelligible.

Certain general indications symbolical of the intended articulation are desirable both in printed speech and in printed boiizationof music-I' is indeed possible to read a poem in articulation is which the lines are not separated from each other, desirable ag -m some ancient writing, and we often read music in which the articulation is not indicated, as in the older classical music; yet in neither case is the reading entirely easy, nor is it always possible to know exactly the meaning of the writer, since diverse articular divisions may make quite different impressions. On the other hand, a book which makes too frequent use of italics, quotation marks, parentheses and punctuation marks is not pleasant and facile reading and, similarly, a piece of music which is over-edited by an excessive use of double-stems, dots, dashes, tenuto marks, slurs, accent marks, dynamic signs, tempo marks, fingerings, and notes of different sizes, is hard to read, and in spite of its multiplied notations still remains incompletely symbolized. The accomplished musician usually advises his pupils to consult and thoroughly to master the different finely edited and annotated publications of the works they are studying, as well as the original edition; although for his own use the master prefers the moderately symbolized original edition, supplementing this with his own originality, feeling, taste, and knowledge, thereby recreating the work, so that in many respects his interpretation differs from that of his peers.

In speech, the connection and the disconnection of words and of syllables are indicated by a close juxtaposition of let-

ters, by spaces, by hyphens, and by diacritical marks; Tne symbois of and similarly, in music, the connection and the. articulation disconnection of tones are indicated by slurs, by tenuto marks, by dots and by vertical dashes placed over or under the notes, by various combinations of these signs applied to the notes, by the absence of all these signs from a note or from a continuous succession of notes, by rests, and by pedal marks. But it must always be remembered that, like all other intended effects, musical articulation is only in small measure symbolized by the composer, who employs the signs only as suggestive guides to the intuition and skill of the player and not as a complete expression of his own intention.

In the proper and expressive rendering of a musical composition, either by means of the voice or by means of a musical instrument, it is necessary to observe pauses of p_-etart0n varying length in order to bring out the meaning Rhetorical and of the writer, just as in compositions where sentential pauses words instead of notes are used as signs of ideas. But the formal punctuation of music is not usually indicated on the printed page in the original works of important composers. Much is left to the judgment and discretion of the reader or performer of the music. However, it is customary for those who annotate special editions of standard works for the use of pupils to supply some of such guiding marks as obviously were understood and observed in the mind of the composer. When, by an editor or a judicious teacher, with print or pencil, marks are added to the original score to suggest the correct mode of punctuation, these auxiliaries usually, instead of being commas, semicolons, and periods, as in common print, are such musical signs as the slur, interlacing slurs, short lines placed singly or in couples across a line of the staff or above the staff, the fermata, the breath-mark, rests, etc. The duration of each of the several pauses should be proportional to the degree of connection between the parts of the musical discourse, and their effective employment depends in great

measure upon the taste, feeling, and imagination of the performer who endeavors to interpret the symbolized message of the composer.

It is exceedingly difficult, if not impossible, by any mode or degree of explanatory notation to supply adequate guidance Audible to him who pursues the path toward superior interpretation musicianship, unillumined by the inner lamp of clear judgment and intuitive sense of fitness. The laws of just proportion apply to all the fine arts, and the correct interpretation of a masterpiece depends upon the same esthetic principle as does the perfect vocal rendering of a masterpiece of literature in artistic recitation. Considerations of tempo, quantity, accent, emphasis, modulation of" tone, grammatical and rhetorical articulation and pause, delicate variation from rigid rules, individuality, continually arise whenever by means of the voice or through the agency of a musical instrument a sensitive singer or player endeavors to reproduce by audible interpretation the inspired conception which lay in the soul of a Bach, a Mozart, a Schubert, and which the master himself inadequately represented in the scores which he may have dashed off in the hurried "rapture of creation." "That a genius like Chopin did not indicate everything accurately is quite explainable," writes Rosenthal. "He flew, where we merely limp after."

Yet we must not undervalue the mechanical aids that it is the office of the competent editor to furnish. As Schumann Schumann's says, "Music would indeed be a miserable art, if words it were able to describe affections only by sounds without language and symbols."

Those modulations of tone termed coloring and shading are largely dependent upon the taste, emotional depth, and poetic vision of the interpreter, and it is of the utmost importance that they should be diversified, natural, and rightly adapted to the subject, for upon them in great measure depends the auditor's enjoyment of the musical performance.

The player's technical command and intuitive feeling are assumed by the composer to be amply sufficient to interpret the written music with convincing musical and poetic art. Absolute departure from the written indications of accredited authorities is not to be tolerated in a beginner, although the master musician, being a law unto himself, while violating no esthetic principle, may disregard musical rules, as a poet may break stereotyped rules of versification, since, as Busoni says, "Thedelivery of a work is a transcription," and "It is for the interpreter to resolve the rigidity of the signs into the primitive emotion."

Intelligent practice of music can proceed only from a full recognition of the elementary principles here briefly discussed. Most of the causes which prevent a correct interpretation of piano music might be suggestive, removed without difficulty providing that music neTer fuUy be considered as an accurate means to a definite end, an art by means of which the soul and the imagination find expression through the voice and instrument, conveying musical thought and feeling in a manner analogous to that by which, through verse, the poet communicates the thoughts, sentiments and aspirations of mankind in the language of words. All notation is suggestive rather than fully elaborated, for the finest shades of interpretation cannot even be suggested by any mechanical contrivance. "All *nuances* cannot be indicated," wrote Beethoven. The musician of breadth and depth comprehends the given signs in their complete significance and in all their relations to the other implied and printed indications, since to him, as to Mendelssohn, "Music is a distinct language." CHAPTER II

Musical Symbols And Their Meaning

The notation used in writing music for the pianoforte might aptly be called musical shorthand. Often representing Musical solely the simplest way of writing a musical shorthand thought, it may also include suggestions in regard to the manner of performance, and the complications and inadequacies of a notation addressing two senses, hearing and touch, and symbolical both of effects

for the ear and of directions to fingers and foot, are among the difficulties with which the pianist contends. Sometimes the sound is more fully expressed by the musical characters than is the mode of execution, and sometimes *vice versa,* the rendition being the same in both cases. As a passage may therefore be notated in many different ways, a thorough and comprehensive knowledge of the language of music is essential in order to perceive from the context the true significance of every note.

It is at times impossible for the composer to write in such a manner that his conception will be disclosed to the pianist

Tonal duration wn S n0 aSo a musici811-In all music the not definitely pitch of a note is absolutely determined by the indicated cie£ preceding it, and in a work composed for orchestral instruments, where each part usually is written on a separate staff, the relative duration of tones is indicated by the notes, and silence by the rests; while the few signs referring to execution are quite definite in their nature. But in a pianoforte composition all the parts, frequently six, eight or more, are compressed upon two staves only, and in the case of an orchestral transcription, or an orchestrally conceived piano composition, a very large number of voices may be represented in the necessarily limited and fewer number of notes which conveniently can be used. It follows that one note may stand for several tones of the same pitch but of varying duration and dynamics, and a developed musical intelligence is necessary to 8 understand its true import; for in written pianoforte music, pitch only is designated with definiteness; signs of tonal duration, release and attack, connection and disconnection are vague, often equivocal, while many of those betokening tonal quantity and quality are not invariable in meaning.

Example 1

a. Original notation.

What couid look simpler than the notes of Example 1 a? Yet the correct way of playing them can be deduced only from an understanding of the idea which they

Diverseread. convey, for the intended duration of the tones ings, synonymous may or may not be fully symbolized. If they be notations written for the violoncello or other orchestral instrument; or for the pianoforte, but imagined as in imitation of an orchestral instrument, they do show the exact duration of the tones; but usually such arpeggiated harmonies form accompaniment to some melody and should not be given as a meager and dry succession of single tones, but so as to sustain all or some of the tones of the harmony, by means of the fingers, the pedal, or both. The full duration of these tones, as usually played, is shown with precision in the two versions at 1 b and 1 c. But it is apparent that a piece notated in either of these ways would be extremely difficult to read, and would not convey the designed meaning nearly so quickly nor so completely as does the ordinary method of writing shown at *a,* which, simple as it is, assumes a certain amount of musical insight and experience on the part of the performer. Besides, even when it is both possible and desirable to point out unmistakably the duration of tones, to do so takes a great deal of the composer's valuable time. Obviously, these three illustrations may typify the same sound; equally true is it that the example at *a* may have diverse authentic readings.

What does a rest mean? Silence? Sometimes; not always. There are sounding rests as well as rests of silence. It constantly happens that although the tone should be held, manual 'the fingers have to be removed from the keys, execution and a rest is written for them, but not for the tone, in which case the notation of the musical conception is complicated with that referring to the execution, the symbols indicating now one, now the other, now both of these, as is shown in the illustration 2 a, taken from Schumann's *Novelette in A major,* in which each bass tone should sound through the measure in the manner shown at 2 b.

Example 2

Schumann — Novelette in A major, Op. 21, No. 6.

a. Original notation. b. The bass, notated as it sounds, and accompanying chords. c. The melody, notated as it sounds. ft J J E J E J E

The notation 2 *b,* more indicative of the desired musical effect than of the means used to produce that effect, calls for the same manner of playing as the original no ,.,.,, ,,, Exact tonal dura tation, both demanding the employment of the tion and pedal damper pedal, as the fingers of the left hand can-execution sym ... ..,,.,. bolized not sustain the bass part while playing the inner parts. Another instance in which the manner of performance is more symbolized than is the sound, occurs in Example 2 *a* in the notes and rests written for the right hand; at c the notes represent the melody as it actually sounds, without specifying whether the tones are sustained by fingers or by pedal. In the original notation, a, the melody of the first two measures is written in quarter-notes, because the keys producing the melodic fib and *C* must be softly struck again by the thumb of the left hand in playing an accompanying voice; but each of these two melodic tones is intended to sound throughout its measure as if written in half-notes. As in the case of the bass, each of these notes of the melody demands the use of the pedal, without which the melodic tones cannot be sustained and connected.

In cases like these there is sometimes an attempt to indicate both the tonal duration desired — a half-note — and the means of producing that duration — the use of signs demanding the pedal — and the composer puts the mark use o£ pedal *Fed.,* as if to say: "The tone should be sustained, even if the fingers cannot do it; the rest is for the fingers, not for the tone." Frequently, however, it is impossible to show by signs either the manual and pedal mode of sustaining a tone without blurring other tones, or the exact moment of pedal release; and so, although the pedal is the chief means of orchestral coloring, often its use is not indicated. When in any voice there is a note of long or of short duration which represents a tone sustained through many measures, the employment of the

pedal is usually left to the judgment of the player. The composer may indicate that the pedal is indispensable by writing under the note to be held the word *Ped.,* without giving a sign for pedal release; or he may employ the phrase *sempre Pedale* (always the pedal); or *Ped. ,* and a little later *sempre simili* (always the same); or, as Schumann often does, *mit Pedal* (with pedal). But, even when not impossible, it remains difficult precisely to designate the exact moments of pedal attack and release, which is one of the reasons why the marks *Ped.* and $ usually are placed incorrectly and are useless as guides to correct pedaling. The conflict between the representation of the sound of the music and of the means by which this sound is produced results Bass notes in form in the adoption of both of these forms of notation of grace-notes m the same composition. This is well illustrated in No. 6 of Schumann's *Bunte Blatter, Op.* 99, where, in each measure, all the chord-notes written for the left hand should be sustained and have the effect of being connected with those in the following measure.
Example 3
Schumann — Bunte Blatter, Op. 99, No. 6.
Where are the bass notes here? This must be known in order to give them the requisite tonal significance as the foundaTo find the tion upon which the. other voices rest. The two bass notes following trials demonstrate without doubt which notes constitute the bass. First, while playing the melody as written, with the left hand sound simultaneously all the other notes of each measure except the first and lowest note, omitting this altogether. Second, play the measures in a similar manner, but omit the second note and hold instead the first note, written as a small note, which can be done by playing some of the chordnotes with the right hand. This mode of playing is at once perceived to be the stronger and more satisfying, proving that the indispensable bass tones lie in the lowest voice. These must be sustained, although represented as grace-notes, and as this can only be done by the pedal, Schumann gives the

general direction, *mit Pedal.*

The second chord-note in each of the first three measures is written as a quarter-note; in each of the next four measures as a dotted half-note: in the last measure as a 111 i-i Quarter-note quarter-note. All these should be sustained as and dotted half-dotted half-notes as nearly as possible. In the note of e«ual fourth, fifth and sixth measures, Schumann writes the notes on the first beat as dotted half-notes, because the player must here sustain and connect them partly by means of the fingers, substituting the fifth finger for the thumb, in order to release the pedal so as to prevent a discordant blurring of the melodic tones C, E and Db, the last tones of each of these measures, with the tone preceding it.

But when the measures are correctly played the pedal is used afresh with each melodic tone as soon as it is connected with the preceding one of different pitch, so that when the fingers are removed from the keys to play the next bass note both the harmony and the melody are sustained and connected to the tones in the next measure. In measure 7, although the dotted half-note is still employed, there is not the same reason for writing it so, as all the melodic tones are also chord-tones.

These examples all show that, unfortunately for the pianist who is not also an experienced musician, the modes by which a desired orchestral or pianistic effect is indicated are numerous. Such confusing variety of notation to express a musical idea is analogous to the mode of spelling in Shakespearean times, when different combinations of letters were admissible in spelling a word.

Transcribers frequently make sad work of pianoforte music. In a certain arrangement for strings, of Schumann's Transcribers' *Childhood Scenes,* a curious mistake occurs. Evimistakes dently the transcriber knew but little of the pecu liarities of notation in pianoforte music. Throughout the piece named *Almost Too Serious (Fast zu ernst),* a few measures of which are given in *Example* 4, the first note of each measure is written as a sixteenth-note, although the composer indicates his desire to have it held as a bass note by writing at the beginning of the piece the word *Ped.* These bass notes were wrongly conceived by the transcriber as intended to be sustained only for their written duration; and so, in adapting them to the violoncello, instead of writing them as connected quarter-notes, he set them down, unchanged, in their pianistic form, as sixteenthnotes. This, bad enough in the first few measures, becomes very unpleasant in effect in the measures where the fermatas occur, as, without the sustained bass, the final harmony becomes a chord of the six-four with which the phrase closes. The transcriber did not conceive correctly the composer's intention that the bass notes should be sustained not merely mentally but audibly and by means of that mechanism which is characteristic solely of the pianoforte — the pedal.

Notes and rests apparently written for a single voice may in reality belong to several voices. And the converse is also true, that notes and rests seemingly written for as several several voices may constitute but a single voice.

These statements are illustrated by the following five musical examples.

Example 5

Bach — Prelude in C Major from *The Well-tempered Clavichord, Part II.*

In the third measure of this Bach *Prelude,* which is written in five independent voices, the notes of the theme, in sixteenths and thirty-seconds, make a single continuous voice, running thread-like through the other voices, which gradually form an accompanying harmony in *C major,* of which the tones C and G enter simultaneously with tones of the same pitch in the theme, and are held much longer than they. To one inexperienced in playing polyphonic music, the notation might be confusing, as, owing to the merging of two voices in the one note, G, written as a quarter-note, the theme seems to stop here, and its continuation in the lower staff appears to the eye to belong to another voice, for the sixteenth-rest (here written for the fingers of the left hand) may give a false impression that the sixteenth-notes in the lower staff are a continuation of the bass voice C. In this example, the quarter-note G, with one stem down-turned, represents both a melody tone of the value of a sixteenth and an accompanying tone four times as long.

In the above *Example,* where one voice is written as several, it is also the case that two voices are represented in one note. Certain measures of the C# *minor Prelude* from *The Well-tempered Clavichord, Part I,* contain similar difficulties and still others, begins with these notes:

Two voices embodied in one note
The *Prelude* Example 6
Bach — C# Minor Prelude.
(meas.1)

Hidden in measure 18, which is given in the next example, is an imitation of this.

Example 7 *a. Imitation of Ex. 6, original notation.*

The melodic imitation at *a* seems, at the first glance, to have lost its first note, and to begin with an eighth-rest; while the dotted half-note E seems to belong to the upper voice only. But the imitation really does begin on the first beat of the measure with an eighth-note, E, which is not given separate notation, but is included in the E written as a dotted half-note, which stands for two voices, not for one as it at first sight may appear to do. Instead of combining these two notes in one, the two E's might have been given separate notation, so as to fully indicate all the notes of both voices, as shown in 7 *b.*

Another feature of interest in the original notation given in *Example 7 a is* that, as in the *C major Prelude,* in *Example 5,* two accompanying tones (C# and Git) enter simultaneously with thematic tones of the same pitch, and are sustained longer than they. This is indicated by the double stems and the slurs. Here again a note with one stem represents two tones belonging to different voices and of differing dynamic qualities as well as differing duration. In this example the rest is neither for the finger nor the tone, but is a sign put to attract the attention of the player to the merging of the thematic E with the E of the highest voice, and also to the entry of the thematic imitation, so that he may bring it out in an interesting manner and with sufficient impressiveness.

Example 8
a. Original notation.

In *Example 8 a,* the notes in the fifteenth measure of the same *Prelude* furnish an illustration of both these ways of writing.' The significance of the notes composing an imitation of the first theme is somewhat concealed by the opposite directions taken by the stems, as well as by the note E doing duty for more than one voice. The lowest voice has *Cft,* which, after a period of rest, descends to a sustained *Aft,* as shown at 8 *b.* The *Fft* on the fourth beat is a continuation of the theme in eighth-notes, as is seen by a comparison of the original notation in *Example 8 a* with that of the theme in *Example 6,* which shows clearly that the F# on the fourth beat and the following *Gft* and *Aft* constitute an inverted free imitation of the thematic notes, *Cft, B* and *A.* usually the clearest

All this is indicated in *Example* 8 *b,* in more detail than in the original notation at *a,* by using more symbols. But, sim lest notation wne the upturned stems, the two E's and the slurs employed make easier an analysis of this measure, yet this notation is less good than that of the original, since it is more complicated in appearance, and therefore not so easy to read.

Examples have been given of one voice written as several, of two voices embodied in one note, and of three voices written several voices as two. It is frequently the case that many written as one voices are represented by a succession of single notes. Thousands of cases could be cited in which arpeggiated (broken) harmonies conceal several voices. One is here given in the variation from the *Andante* of Beethoven's *F minor Sonata, Op.* 57, where the notes on the upper staff, at 9 *a,* stand for three voices.

Example 9
Beethoven — Sonata, Op. 57, Andante, Var. 2.

a. Original notation.

This is attested by *Example 9 b,* in which the notes represent the same harmony as those at 9 *a,* but in solid instead of arpeggiated chords. If these two examples be played, this is unmistakably heard.

Yet that an arpeggiated chord does not always represent more than one voice is shown by the opening measures of the Bach *Prelude,* of which the third measure is cited Musical judgin *Example* 5. In the first two measures of this ment necessary *Prelude,* shown below, there is but one melodic voice, although this is constructed more from chords than from the scale. It is obvious that musical judgment is necessary to discriminate between an arpeggiated passage representing several voices and one representing but a single part.

Example 10 Bach—Well-tempered Clavichord, Prelude 1 from Part II.

The dot as accent; as staccato mark; to indicate sustained tone

Not only do notes, rests and stems all have more than one meaning, but so, also, have other musical symbols. The dot placed above or below a note has various meanings. It often calls for some quality of staccato — a shortening of the note above or below which it is placed. It may demand a heavy, orchestral staccato or a light finger staccato; it may mean that the detachment of one tone from another should be like a breath, a sigh, or may call for a pronounced rest between two tones, such as is usually demanded by the vertical dash placed above a note. At times the dot calls for a non-legato touch; or it may signify that the notes are to be played in imitation of a violin pizzicato. Often the dot is used, not as a staccato mark, but as an accent mark or a mark of emphasis, the tenuto mark being comparatively a modern sign. Beethoven often uses the dot in this way, and Bulow, in his instructive editions, frequently employs it with the same meaning. It may even be used to call the attention of the eye to the fact that the note under or over which it is placed should be long sustained — witness especially the compositions of Chopin, Schumann and Liszt.

And there are other characters which may cause confusion. When the notation is involved, the accent mark (A) is some,,.... times used to call attention to a succession of

Meanings of the accent mark; of interesting tones in an inner voice, or merely *the* slur to a note of long duration, which must be so attacked as to sound for a sufficiently long time. The primary use of the slur is to signify that the notes included within its curve should be played smoothly, connectedly, and without attack — *i.e.,* legato. It is sometimes used to group together notes of a melody hard to find because interlaced with notes of other voices, or because they are found now on the upper staff, now on the lower, as in the third measure of *Example 2 a,* where it is also used to indicate an alternate use of the hands. And some editors (not composers) use it as a sign of phrasing.

It has been shown that the duration of a tone is not indicated in the notation so as to make but one interpretation posc sible; that a rest may demand cessation of tone, summary. " incompleteness or merely a rest for the finger while the tone conof notation tinues, or it may be used to attract attention to an important succeeding note or passage. It is demonstrated that the notes of one voice may appear to the inexperienced player to belong to several voices or to the wrong voice; also, that several voices may simultaneously employ the same note or rest, or other sign; that a note with one stem may symbolize one voice or many voices of differing duration and tonecolor; that a note with two stems may symbolize two or more parts, and that the upward or downward direction of the stem may have significance either for the hand or for the tone. Also, it is obvious that a note written in small size, or as a grace-note, may be long sustained and of great melodic or harmonic value; that neither the dot, the accent mark nor the slur is limited to a single significance, and that the use of the pedal is not definitely indicated.

The question naturally arises: Would it not simplify the notation, without detracting from the ease of writing, read-

ing or playing the music, if each sign should always Many meanings imply but one meaning? But these many signs of each symbol for the same manner of playing and the numerous meanings of each character are the outcome of centuries of musicwriting, an art which, like that of music itself, has been long in process of evolution, and bears the impress of the conventional usage of many different periods, each composer using the signs with which he is most familiar, and which appeal to him as simplest, most lucid and most effective to represent his musical ideas; although the selection is in the main instinctive, not thought out, for, with a few notable exceptions, composers concern themselves but little with the manner in which they write down their thoughts. Then, too, much of the confusion in musical writing comes through a misunderstanding of Italian musical terms by those who do not speak the language. Even good musicians have unconsciously used signs incorrectly in their compositions, and in time many of these corruptions have become authoritative usage; hence we now have many correct interpretations of each symbol. It is best not to trust too much to signs but rather to look through the sign to its meaning as determined not only by other signs with which it is combined but by the composition itself.

Through comparison of different editions of a composition the pianist becomes able to make his own edition; that is, he learns to interpret such signs as occur with far more accuracy than they can possibly be written, editions, indeand to see the true meaning of any composition, *wem* 0f no matter how badly edited it may be; and thus he attains to a feeling for correct ways of playing — correct ways — for there is no one way right and all others wrong, but many which are correct. The manner of execution depends much upon the rendering of preceding passages, as well as upon the pianist's general style. As the study of many compositions by the same composer gives ideas as to his distinctive characteristics, it is desirable to study-simultaneously several pieces by the same composer; some in good editions, some in poor editions, that they may be compared and the judgment exercised as to the best reading. Therefore, in order thoroughly to understand any one composition, it is well to study it in the original edition or in some unannotated edition, as well as in the fine editions arranged by Liszt, Bulow, Klindworth, Busoni, d'Albert, Mugellini, Buonamici and other good musicians. A comparison of texts facilitates the formation of a correct conception of the meaning of the composer. One may become in a certain sense a pupil of Liszt or of Bulow by carefully studying the signs and comments added to the original edition. The drawback to such instruction is that the writer cannot adapt himself to the special needs of the pupil. To foster independent j udgment and prevent a mechanical adoption of his own conception, Bulow forbade the use of his editions to his own pupils, preferring to correct their misconceptions and their errors of taste through personal instruction.

But even such comparison of editions will not fully give the pianist an understanding of the compositions he studies. SomeKnowledge of thing more is necessary to enable him to use the theory texts understandingly. Without much hearing of good music of all kinds, and without a knowledge of harmony, counterpoint, rhythm and musical form, the pianist may be unable to discriminate between the notation representing the sound and that suggesting the execution; he may even be unconscious of the need to do this.

In either case he must be dependent upon a guide, and remain in pupilage so long as his ignorance continues; whereas The musician-the musician-pianist reads the meaning through pianist the notation; his correct conception insures correct playing. Add to this a poetic temperament, and he is capable of artistic interpretation.

CHAPTER III

Bowing-signs

Symbols are arbitrary signs for things that are not arbitrary. Much of the symbolization of articulation is the same in all music, whether it be written for voice or for instru-weai tone ment. Consequently it is helpful as well as consymbolized venient, when discussing the interpretation of music written for one kind of instrument, that both the interpretation and the mode of execution should be described in terms which, when applied in their original, limited meaning, are suitable only to music written for some other kind of instrument. *Portamento, sotto voce, cantabile, legato, pizzicato,* and *downbeat* are terms originating in vocal and orchestral music; yet some of these are frequently seen in the notation of piano music and others are in common verbal use by pianists. And rightly so; for since the conceived tone should be more expressive than it is possible to render the tone actually brought forth by the player, such vocal and orchestral terms are more potent in the production of an ideal musical conception and a consequent fine musical rendering than matter-of-fact terms which can be taken literally. Since all great composers are writers of vocal and of orchestral music, and, therefore, with few exceptions, often feel, think and write orchestrally for the piano, it is requisite, in order to understand the meaning of the notation for the piano, to have some elementary knowledge of the notation for the voice and for orchestral instruments.

Next in importance to the poetic content of the work, and essentially a preconsideration, is its musical significance. Correctly to interpret this, it is imperative that the MusicaIand musical significance of each symbol be understood executionai imexactly and that this be absolutely differentiated portof symb0ls from its executional import, which varies with each musical medium. These two distinctly separate functions should be realized as absolutely different in kind; and the musical significance, which is of universal application because of its appertaining to ideal musical sound, is the broader. In the light of this truth, it is apparent that the piano is merely one of the many mediums of musical expression. Most of its symbols were first employed in vocal and in orchestral music.

Explanations of the symbols and terminology used in pianoforte music are in many important works confused by the writers with the means of execution—the touch of the fingers. All signs and all terminology, such as slur, dot, dash, accent mark, phrase, punctuation, staccato and legato, should first be understood in their original and truest significance, as symbolizing ideal musical effect; after which, the special manner of producing the effect on each kind of instrument should also receive careful consideration, since the signs not only represent the sound but also instruct as to the means of execution. The mechanical means of interpretation used—the fingers, wrist, hand, arm, shoulder and foot—and the part they take in setting into action the very complicated mechanism of the piano, should in no way affect the ideal conception of the sound to be produced.

Faulty instruction similar to the following, clipped from a recent music journal, appears to be very common: "There are Legato, but two ways of playing the piano—legato and staccato staccato; hence they should be rightly understood and correctly used. In the legato, the hand is quiet and the finger moves. In the staccato, the finger is quiet and the hand moves.... A slow staccato or legato may also involve arm action." A study of the playing of distinguished pianists shows that both staccato and legato are produced by the finger alone, as well as by the added employment of hand, forearm and upper arm; the touch depending very largely upon the quality of tone desired—its richness, dryness, delicacy, power, brilliance, resonance or purity. But the musical meaning of legato and of staccato has to do only with tonal connection, disconnection, attack and lack of attack. The manner of execution is an entirely different matter, depending upon the instrument employed and upon the conception of the performer; and the interpretation of a great player varies somewhat with each performance, in response to the inspiration of the moment.

In the *Novum Organum,* Bacon states

the profound and farreaching principle that "No one successfully investigates the nature of anything in itself; the inquiry must be How to enlarged, so as to become more general." It investigate therefore becomes necessary, in order to understand the significance of the symbols found in music written for the piano, that their significance should be perceived in music written for other instruments, since a similar musical intention is represented, regardless of the mechanism of the instrument which may be the chosen medium of interpretation.

The necessity of a feeling for orchestral coloring is plainly evident to him who reads carefully the annotations of eminent editors of pianoforte music. D 'Albert writes in orchestration his edition of Beethoven's sonatas: "This part of piano music might well be instrumented; here imitate the tone of the flute, and four bars further on, that of the reeds." "Imagine the upper voice in these two bars played by the oboe, and the accompaniment performed by the strings." "Imitate the sound of harmonics on the harp." "Like a brass band, the left hand subduing its part played pizzicato." "Recall the sound of the trombone." "Quasi clarinetto." Billow, also, indicates the desirability of orchestral thinking on the part of the pianist, by such comments as: "Sound *C-F* shrill like a trumpet-call here; at *b* like a drum beat." "Imagine this passage thus orchestrated:—the violins and flutes should take *E,* while *D* is doubtless conceived for the natural trumpet and corresponds perfectly with its character." "The pianist should study the tone of the low violoncello strings." In order to investigate the nature of certain signs used in the notation of piano music, the inquiry will be enlarged by a comparison with the notation used in violin music, Berlioz's and for that purpose a glimpse of the notation used "marks for the violin, as explained by Berlioz in his treatise, *Modern Instrumentation and Orchestration,* is here presented, these comments and illustrations being pertinent to the discussion.

"The different kinds of bowing are of great importance, and exercise a singular influence on the sonorousness and the expression of peculiar features and melodies. They should therefore be carefully indicated—according to the nature of the idea which is to be conveyed—by the following signs:

"For *detached* notes:

"For *staccato* or *lightly detached* notes, simple or double, which are to be executed during a single drawing of the bow, by means of a succession of small j erks advancing as little as possible:

Allegro

"For *markedly detached* notes, which are to give to the string all possible sonorousness, by permitting it to vibrate alone after the bow has vigorously struck it, and which particularly suit pieces of a haughty, grand character, and of moderate movement:

"The undulating tremolo-consists of a not very rapid utterance of two bound notes on the same tone; while the bow never quits the string. Gluck wrote thus:

Among other things the above citations call attention to the suggestive fact that the dots in the first staff are to be indicated "for *detached* notes," while those in the sixth staff, identical in appearance and placed over notes of the same value, are to be indicated "for *markedly detached* notes, which are to give to the string all possible sonorousness." Evidently tempo and other musical requirements enter into the meaning of the dot.

The slur and its various combinations with the dot, as instanced by Berlioz, are employed also in music written for wind instruments, where similar effects of connection, disconnection and attack of sound are meaning produced by means of the breath; and they are ofsiurand frequently met with in piano music, where they have the same musical purport. The musical purport is exactly the same, although the mechanical means employed in the execution of notes written for the piano is neither the breath, controlled by throat, lip and tongue and applied to a tube of air, nor the bow, controlled by fingers, wrist and arm, and applied directly to the strings, but consists of keys controlled by the fingers, which indirectly, by means of levers, apply hammers and dampers to the strings, thereby eliciting and checking tone, and of pedals, the functions of which are discussed in Chapter XII.

Musical tones are produced by exciting the air to regularly recurrent vibration, by means of vibrating strings, of vibrating columns of air or of any other periodically vi-various offices brating body. All instrumentalists use their of the fingers fingers in producing tone, employing them in different ways. In playing the harp the fingers directly incite the vibration of the strings; in playing wind instruments the fingers are mainly employed to define the pitch of the vibration which is incited by the breath; and in playing bowed stringed instruments the fingers of the right hand hold the bow, which is the vibration-producing medium, while the fingers of the left hand determine the pitch. But in playing the piano the fingers do not perform their office nearly so directly, since there intervene between them and the strings three important mechanisms, controlled by many lesser ones. Finger pressure upon a key produces tone from a single string or from two or three unison strings by means of indirectly moving to action; the damper which lies upon, and the hammer which rests about one and three-quarters of an inch below the string or strings. The sensitive finger-tip must control judiciously these various mechanisms which intervene between it and the strings.

"There are three grades in musical rendition," says Hans von IJulow. "One can play correctly, beautifully, interestingly. To attain to a Now do not play so interestingly that it ceases to correct be correct!" "A correct execution is exactly conception equivalent to a fine one. " "To play correctly, one must make it impossible for oneself to play incorrectly. 'r Not only does piano playing become infinitely more delightful when comparisons are made, mentally, of vocal and orchestral with pianoforte music,but by so doing it eventually becomes impossible to conceive the music incorrectly, which is a long step toward masterly performance. Close study of the strings, especially, is productive of a clearer musical insight. Many a passage, the conception of which may be hazy and uncertain to the pianist, becomes entirely comprehensible when he pauses to imagine how it should be rendered, vocally or orchestrally, how it would be arranged for string quartet and how the players would bow it.

Sometimes the new application of an old sign, retaining its primary musical meaning, but not its executional meaning as Busoni's down-intended only for one kind of instrument, is of bow mark immense value in clarifying the notation. A most vivid illustration of this is to be found in *AW Italia,* the second piece in Busoni's *Elegien,* in which he employs the violin sign for the down-bow, i—i, to indicate the desired attack and the strongly syncopated character of a note. No one of the usual ways of marking would have made so clear his intention as to the rendering of the passage.

Bowing-signs

For the furtherance of his musical development, as well as of his pleasure, the interest and attention of the pianist should be strongly attracted to the strings, because of all orchestral instruments they are the most important, possessing, as they do, the most beautiful as well as the most varied qualities. And also because the means employed by the singer or by the player upon a wind instrument to express the music is not apparent to the eye, since the medium which incites the air to vibration is the invisible breath; but the medium by which the violinist incites the air to vibration is the visible bow, the down and up movements of which are easily seen, even from a distance. For all of these reasons, if the comprehensive terms "bowing-signs" or "signs of bowing" were adopted by pianists in discussing and in explaining to students the significance of the slur and of the staccato dot and dash, it is possible that the general musical understanding might become much clearer and more intelligent, and the pitiful helplessness in regard to the meaning of these signs which. is evinced by some of the questions and

answers of teachers in leading music journals might easily be relieved. The strangeness of the term *bowing-signs* as applied to piano music would vanish as soon as its breadth of meaning, as determining with definiteness the musical significance of certain symbols, was understood; and if seen in written discourse and heard from the tongue of the teacher, like Busoni's down-bow mark, and like the more frequently used *sotto voce, cantabile, pizzicato,* etc., it would soon seem a perfectly natural and a very exact term of expression. The terms *bowing-signs* and *signs of bow-, ing* are here used as comprehending the several signs of alltication. Experience in teaching pianists has shown the term "bowing-signs" to be a useful one. By its employment all confusion of articulation with phrasing is avoided, while slurs, dots and their combinations lose their terrors for the student.

The principal bowing-signs are the slur embracing within its curve two or more notes, the slur embracing within its The bowing-curve notes of which one or more may be marked signs with a dot, the dot or dash placed over or under a note or each of a succession of notes, and notes marked by the absence of slur, dot and dash.

There are relatively few pianists of moderate accomplishment who rightly interpret the meaning of the slur, either used siur a sign of alone or in combination with the dot, although le8ato this is fundamentally important and quite definite. This is because, although the slur is used by composers as a bowing-sign demanding legato and for no other purpose, this legato sign is sometimes placed over the notes of a motive or other integral subdivision of a phrase, as is shown in *Example* 18. But in such cases, also, the slur is used as a sign of legato, not as an indication of phrasing, which the composer rarely tries to indicate by special signs. He does not use slurs to define the limits of phrases and sentences, and it is the bringing out of the relationships of these that constitutes phrasing in the truest meaning of the word. The slur, then, is used to group together notes which are to be

rendered legato.

The slur is not used as a punctuation mark by renowned composers, either of the past or of the present, as can be seen by consulting the works of Beethoven, xhesiumota Schumann, Chopin, MacDowell, Strauss, Debussy "Mrk of phasing or other preeminent authorities. Any sign employed with a meaning different from what has long been used and continues to be used by the best composers is not to be considered as applying with a newly given signification to the works of masters who use this sign with the meaning sanctioned by the use of centuries. Even if the change in the meaning of the sign should be a desirable one, it becomes authoritative only after its acceptance and employment by the best composers of the day; and even then it cannot apply to compositions written before the invention of the newly given meaning.

As a mark of punctuation the slur is used only in the extremely valuable and interesting editions of Dr. Hugo Riemann and in those of his followers. There is not one ,,,_,,._,, ,,,,

Riemann s use of important modern composer who has adopted the slur as mark of Riemann notation. All continue to employ the phrasmg slur, as did the classic writers, as a sign of legato, not of phrasing. Legato consists in the smooth, unattacked binding of one tone to another. Absence of attack is absolutely necessary to a true legato. In pianoforte playing each tone is produced by means of a hammer striking upon strings, and the term *legato* as applied to this instrument must therefore mean: Obtain legato as nearly as is possible, that is, with as little attack and as much connection of tone as is compatible with the nature of this percussive instrument. Even staccato tones can be made to sound legato if produced with a minimum of attack; while the most connected tones will not sound legato if they are attacked, since the percussion of the hammer upon the strings makes a quicker and more vivid impression upon the ear than does the connection of tones which takes place simultaneously with the blow, and the effect upon the auditor is that of disconnection of tone. Therefore, no matter what the intention of the performer, or what the technical means employed, wherever the binding of tones ceases to *sound* perfectly connected and unattacked, there the legato ceases. Legato is most perfectly produced by the singer when vocalizing upon a vowel. The most perfect and the most beautiful instrumental legato is produced by the bowed string instruments, which are capable of sustaining the legato indefinitely, and the playing of Kubelik or of the Flonzaley Quartet teaches the pianist more about legato than can the playing of any pianist.

Incorrect statements regarding the slur are constantly met with in books on piano playing and in works on the technic of incorrect state-the instrument; and errors are perpetuated by ments in books tne reliance of pianists and of teachers upon these works, and their consequent belief in, and restatement to pupils of, basic falsities. The following quotations from a music journal are open to criticism upon this point.

"Our pianoforte music contains two kinds of slurs; one kind the composer placed as they appear, the other the enSome printed graver put in where he thought they should emerrors bellish the page. In other words, what I call *conventional* slurs, which do not mean punctuation; and *real slurs,* which do. The conventional slurs generally, cover a natural rhythmic group, such as a single pulsation, a measure, a half-measure, — more often a measure. These slurs are without value as punctuation. Any slur which stops before the notes which really complete the idea, is incorrectly placed and conventional, and not to be regarded except in its permanent value, which is to adjure a legato of the tones covered by it. All slurs mean this. ... The following will be helpful: Any slur which covers a rhythmic group ending with an unaccented tone is conventional and implies simply legato; and a slur connecting parts of two different rhythmic groups (pulses, measures) is punctuational." "Should you go further and ask me why the slurs are drawn incorrectly in printed music, I answer that

is one of the things no fellow can find out."

It is an unfortunate misconception of the significance of the slur to think that it is merely a "conventional" sign. Imagine, for example, Beethoven, who was so slurnot thoughtfully precise and painstaking in his no-"conventional" tation, as being so unintelligent and so foolish as sign constantly and throughout his entire life to permit his works; to be published containing thousands of signs which he had not written in his manuscript and which were absolutely incorrect. No: the conventional he could not tolerate. He was most particular that all signs written by him' should be printed exactly as they stood in the manuscript, and he frequently complains, in' his letters to engravers and to copyists, of their mistakes. He writes to a copyist concerning one of the last great string-quartets, — that in *A minor, Op.* 132: "For Heaven's sake, impress on Kempel to copy everything as it stands; look carefully over my present corrections and you will find all that you have to say to him. When ' is put over a note,' is not to take its place, and *vice versa.* It is not the same thing to write... » r r r w r r f

The slurs to be just as they are placed. It is not synonymous to write I,, m J *mz* =: or thus:

Such is our will and pleasure! I have passed no less than the whole forenoon today, and yesterday afternoon, in correcting these two pieces, and I am actually quite hoarse from stamping: and swearing." Upon another occasion he writes: "I have looked over the whole of the parts... and I trust they must be tolerably correct." There is no reason to assume that Beethoven would not have been equally exacting in his demands in regard to the engraving of his pianoforte works, and it is inconceivable that the corrections so urgently called for were not made. Misprints in music are all too frequent, yet slurs are not more often incorrectly placed than are other signs.

It is quite true, as stated in the quotation from the music journal, that most slurs are not punctuational,—do not indicate Legato slurs the phrasing, — but

do indicate the legato, and important ag used by the composer this is their only office, except when used in combination with other bowing-signs. Legato slurs, however, are most important, are usually correctly placed, and are not in the least conventional nor in any way to be disregarded, since every sign is of moment, as showing in a general way the intention of the composer.

Attendance, score in hand, at orchestral and chamber concerts, where playing of the strings may be observed, forces The violinist's *on* the auditor the perception that the first note legato-bowing within a slur bears the attack of the bow, and hence that this note is by nature more pronounced than those which follow in the same bow. Consequently, the beginning of a slur is often placed over a note which for some reason the composer may wish attacked or accented. Usually, unless the violinist takes pains to prevent it, the legato is destroyed whenever a down-bow is succeeded by an up-bow, or an up-bow is succeeded by a down-bow. Sometimes it is the composer's desire to have the legato extend over several slurred groups of notes — more notes than the player can possibly take in one bow. Quite often a different notation occurs for the same effect, the composer placing under one slur more notes than can be bowed together, with the intention, as before, that the performer shall make them all sound legato. Not infrequently Beethoven employs this manner of indicating his desire for a legato of many notes. To accomplish such an effect the musically undesired but mechanically necessary change of direction in which the strings are bowed must be inaudible and almost imperceptible. Yet it should be remembered in such cases, as always, that, in common with other symbols, slurs are guides only to the general effect desired, and unindicated articular subdivisions are frequently divined and executed by the performer, even in slurred passages.

Although good pianists think and speak of legato as the fundamental touch to be acquired, yet they are always conscious of the attack of the hammer on the strings, — it is characteristic of the instrument,—but fine players attain to such skill that ab will the sound of the attack is reduced to a mini-The pianists mum. In playing legato, the lifelong difficulty lesato with which the violinist struggles — avoidance of attacked tone when taking a new bow—has its counterpart in the pianist's struggle to avoid attacking each tone produced. While the competent pianist greatly reduces the effect of attack, yet he can never really produce legato tones on his instrument, since each tone is produced by the striking of a hammer upon the string instead of by drawing a bow continuously across it. Of course, the pianist utilizes the characteristic hammer-attack of the strings for suitable musical purposes.

We are compelled to differ with many of the statements regarding pianoforte notation made in that standard authority, Grove's Dictionary, including portions of the Errors in Grove's following quotations from the articles "Legato," Dictionary "Slur" and "Phrasing." "Legato consists in the sound of each note of a phrase being sustained until the next is heard. Hn singing a legato passage is vocalized upon a single vowel, on stringed instruments by a single stroke of the bow, and on the pianoforte and organ by keeping the finger upon its key until the exact moment of striking the next.... The slur is now used in a more restricted sense, to denote a special phrasing effect, in which the last of the notes within the curved line is shortened and a considerable stress laid on the first." "The signs which govern the connection or disconnection of the sounds are the dash or dot, and the curved line indicating legato. The ordinary use of these signs has already been described, and the due observance of them constitutes a most essential part of phrasing, but in addition to this the curved line is used to denote an effect of peculiar importance, called the *Slur*.... When the curved line is drawn over two notes of considerable length, or in slow tempo, it is not a slur, but merely a sign of legato, and the same if it covers a group of three or

more notes. In this there is no curtailment of the last note."

Since attack nullifies legato, it is more correct to say that in piano-playing as in violin-playing, legato consists in the unattacked connection of two or more successive tones. The last of the notes comprised within the slur may or may not be shortened; and a considerable stress may or may not be laid on the first note. This depends upon the performer's conception of the passage and of the modes of articulation and pronunciation best adapted to enunciate the musical syllables each in its due proportion to the whole. There must be orchestral as well as pianistic conception of legato, also of the varying degrees and qualities of detachment and of attack, by whatsoever names these may be designated—of *nonlegato, semi-staccato, mezzo-staccato, martellato-staccato, spiccato, pizzicato, rests*. All are effects natural to and inherent in bowed instruments, which often should be imitated in piano-playing, if a passage be conceived correctly. The term *"martellatolegato"*—hammered legato—although inaccurate, is most useful, as implying attacked but connected tones; but this is not true legato. The star is, of course, a sign, and not an "effect." Although occasionally the slur defines the limits of a phrase-subdivision, it is not used by composers for that purpose, but as a sign of legato—a bowing-sign, not a sign of punctuation. The due observance of legato and staccato "constitutes a most essential part of phrasing," in a way somewhat similar to that in which the connection and disconnection of syllables might be considered as constituting a part of phrasing in ordinary language. A correct articulation is, of course, a rudimentary necessity. It is to be regretted that the musical examples given in Grove's Dictionary in the article "Phrasing" are illustrative, not of phrasing, but of legato, staccato and accent.

"In pianoforte music, all passages which are without any mark are played legato, inasmuch as the notes are not detached; the curved line is therefore more for the sake of giving a finished appear-

ance to the passage than from any practical necessity."

Here are several serious and misleading errors. It is obvious that a "finished appearance" is of no moment to the composer. His aim is to convey to others certain of his feelings and ideas. The various signs which he places on paper are intended to convey his musico-poetic meaning, precisely as written words convey the meaning of the poet. The expression of his inspiration is the only purpose of the poet, in music as in letters. Neither writes any sign for the sake of embellishing paper.

Passages of notes marked by the absence of slur, dot and dash are by no means "always played legato," although phrases which are songful in character should of course be Absence *ot* slur played legato and as much as possible in imitation in legato of the voice or of a stringed instrument, whether or passage not the notes be marked by slurs. Yet, as can be seen in many piano compositions, unslurred notes may demand a legato rendering. A good example of this is to be found in the original edition of Beethoven's *F minor Sonata, Op.* 57. The melodynotes from the slow movement, given below, are not marked by slurs, because their cantabile character is so pronounced that it does not need to be pointed out by the composer. As Billow remarks, the legato "is here a matter of course." Example 12

Beethoven—Sonata, Op. 57. Andante.

In violin-music, the bowing-sign, indicated by the absence of slur, dot and dash, calls for detachment of tone, and each of the notes so marked is played in a separate bow. The absence of these signs in piano-music does not marked by always call for detachment of tone, as has been absence of slur, seen. But when, as is very often the case, such notes constitute passage-work; or when, as in quartets and in trios for the piano and strings, identical or similar passages, perhaps thematic or imitative in character, are found alternately in the several parts for the strings and in the part for the piano, then, naturally, these passages represent an identical or a similar musical conception, the several manners of execution varying according to the mechanism of the instrument employed. So that, in such passages, not only the players on the bowed-instruments, but the pianist, also, plays as the musical context of the piece may demand and not according to some arbitrary method devised only for pianists and implying that the essence of pianoforte music differs from that of all other music. "There are many passages in Beethoven's works," writes Schindler, "which, though not marked with slurs, require to be played legato. But this a cultivated taste will instinctively perceive." This statement implies that legato passages are most frequently marked with slurs, and that unslurred notes are usually to be played in a detached manner.

As Beethoven was peculiarly exact and minute in his notation, musical examples illustrative of detached notes marked by the absence of dot and dash will be drawn from his pianoforte sonatas. Annotated by distinguished musicians and pianists such as Hans von Billow and Eugen d'Albert, are editions invaluable in forming the understanding of the developing pianist.

Example 13

Beethoven—Sonata, Op. 31, No. 3. Presto.

Of the preceding measures, taken from the last movement of Beethoven's *Sonata in E, Op. 31, No. 3,* Billow remarks: "The prevailing style of touch in this movement having to be *non legato* (midway between legato and staccato), fingerings may be chosen which facilitate the action of the fingers."

"The undulating figure in sixteenth-notes should be played by both hands with a distinctly detached touch in the successive fingers, *i.e.,* 'non legato,'" says the same editor, of these measures from the *C major Sonata, Op.* 53.

"Do not play the figures with an extreme legato," says Billow of the above measures taken from the slow movement of the *Sonata in F minor, Op.* 57. "What is called the 'pearly touch' is peculiarly appropriate here." Example 16

Beethoven — Sonata, Op. 110. Moderate.

a. Original edition.

Concerning these measures from the first movement of the *Sonata in A, Op.* 110, Billow says: "Here also the notes not especially marked must be played *non legato";* and d'Albert in his edition makes the comment: "The editor plays the first note *staccatissimo,* the remaining three notes *non legato. "* In Billow's edition the notation of the articulation is amplified by additional bowing-signs, as shown by the slurs at *b.*

Of the following measures from the last movement of the *Sonata, Op.* Ill, Billow says: "In the original edition the slur ends here. It is evident that a close legato is not compatible with the *sforzatos* prescribed for the weak beat. On the other hand, avoid an unesthetic hammering and thumping, — to which end we have added *meno legato. "*

As has been shown, the different bowings produce either legato or some degree of attack and of detachment of tones. When uncertain how to interpret a piano passage, it is often helpful to think of it as rendered by the orchestra. Concentrated, thoughtful listening to this imaginary orchestral effect — meanwhile feeling, hearing and noting the instrumentation and judging also as to the probable manner of the bowing employed by the strings—usually leads the pianist to a correct conception of an execution which will interpret the various signs.

Of bowing-slurs in the first movement of the *Sonata in A major, Op.* 101, Billow wrote: "The employment of doubled slurs may confuse some readers; it is to be explained thus: are to be played *F$-E* in the i, /, ;. j -j. Bowing-slurs means that *G#-F#* in an ordinary legato, and less connected manner comand designated by dots under monly termed portamento a slur. But the following mode of notation might also be chosen:- Hvtts" though it could likewise be misunderstood, that of whereas the original mode, derived from bowed-instruments, is familiar to all violinists."

All symbols, whether of speech or of music, are relative, not absolute in meaning. Most of the details of performance must be determined by the per-

former, since the Editorial composer cannot spend his inspired hours in elaboration elaborately editing his works. Besides, even if he were to make an attempt to put on paper signs for every small detail of performance, much would necessarily still remain unindicated, for complete notation of the composer's conception is an impossibility. The slur, therefore, is an arbitrary sign used to indicate, *in a general way only,* the legato of tones. The next four examples illustrate this.

Example 18

Beethoven — Sonata, Op. 54. In tempo d'un Menuetto.

a. Original edition.

The above measures of melody taken from the first movement of the *F major Sonata, Op.* 54, are shown in four editions, Klindworth's edition subdivides the notes under the original long slur into three slurred groups, and places dots over several of the notes. Billow's edition subdivides the notes differently, even extending the first short slur of the original over five notes instead of three, and making three groups of slurred notes where the original edition has two groups, explaining that, "while the left hand plays an unbroken legato, the division of the slur in the highest part will form no unsuitable variant." D'Albert adds accent marks and lengthens the slur to include two of the original slurs. These various editorial marks merely amplify the original notation. All of these editions are correct, each representing the taste and judgment of an authoritative interpreter.

Example 19, taken from the slow movement of the *C minor Sonata, Op.* 13, gives the original notation at *a.* At *b* is given Billow's notation of the same measures, showing added dots to notes in the upper staff; additional stems, slurs and dots to notes in the lower staff; and a different placing of a longer slur in both staves. Here the articulation is notated in more detail than in the original edition. Example 20

Beethoven — Sonata, Op. 13. Rondo.

a. Original edition. b. Biilow edition.

As is seen in *Example* 20, the original notation at *a* is amplified in the Billow edition at *b* by additional tenuto-marks, dots and a slur.

Example 21

Beethoven — Sonata, Op. 10, No. 2. Allegro.

a. Original edition.

The slurs in *Example* 21 *a,* from the first movement of the *Sonata in F major, Op.* 10, may be elaborated as in the notation at *b,* without violating the meaning of the original notation. *Examples* 16, 18, 19, 20, 21 illustrate at *a* the original bowing-signs as written by the composer, to indicate, approximately, his intentions regarding the connection and disconnection of notes. The more minute articular indications added by the various editors, each according to his particular interpretation of the notation, are in no case contradictory to the meaning of the original notation.

"The quintessence of our thoughts," writes Wagner, "is unconveyable in direct ratio as they gain in depth and compass." Says Rubinstein: "I hold that music is a Ian-subjective guage, — to be sure of a hieroglyphic tone, — interpretation image, character; one must first have deciphered the hieroglyphics; then only, however, he may read all that the composer intends to say, and there remains only the more particular indication of the meaning.—. the latter is the task of the interpreter.... Every interpretation, if it is made by a person and not a machine, is *co ipso* subjective. To do justice to the object (the composition) is the law and duty of every interpreter, but of course each one in his own way, that is, subjectively— and how is any other imaginable? There are no two persons of the same character, the same nervous system, the same physical complexion; even the differences of touch of the piano players, of the tone of violin and 'cello players, and the quality of the voice in singers, of the nature of the director, affect the subjective in interpretation.... Should the conception of a composition be objective, there could be only *one* right one, and all executants would be obliged to accommodate themselves to it — what would an executive artist be in that case? A monkey?. .. Should it be different in the interpre-

tation of music than it is in the art of acting? Is there only *one* correct art of Hamlet or King Lear? and must each actor only hope to ape *one* Hamlet or *one* King Lear in order to do justice to the subject? Ergo, I can only allow of the subjective in the interpretation of music. " Josef Hofmann relates that his master often said to him: "Do you know the difference between piano-playing and piano-reciting? Piano-playing is the movement of the fingers; piano-reciting is the movement of the soul." CHAPTER IV

Phrasing

The musical intelligence of the pianist is supposed to be sufficient to perceive, without signs of punctuation, The intelligent the limits and the relations of the various pianist sentences and phrases. The composer assumes that the player is able to subdivide the phrase properly into its integral members and to articulate suitably the short syllabic tone-groups and single tones of which they are composed. Only by considerable stretching of the real meaning of phrasing can the members of a phrase be considered under that term, since these do not express a thought, but are merely correctly assembled tone-groups, each expressing a short and very incomplete portion of a musical thought. Still, as these subdivisions of a phrase are commonly treated under phrasing, they will be here so considered.

As in language, so in music, the phrases composing a work are made to assume their proper relation to each A phrase not other and to the whole composition by a necessarily suitable employment of articulation, accent,

Iegat0 emphasis, shading and coloring, and especially by sentential and rhetorical pauses. A musical phrase may be composed of legato tones or of staccato tones or of any combination of legato and of detached tones. A musical phrase or a phrase-member is not of necessity articularly detached from adjoining sentential divisions, since entire sentences may be sounded either staccato or legato. It is somewhat the same in speech: consider the staccato utterance of Mrs. Fiske and the musical legato of

the lines delivered by Mme. Bernhardt.

Sentential subdivision beginning in middle of slurred group of notes

This passage from Billow's edition of the Beethoven *Sonata, Op. 81a,* is of interest as authoritatively recording an instance of what occurs in innumerable instances; namely, that a phrase or one of its integral subdivisions may begin on any note whatsoever, and regardless of the signs of bowing. There may be many bowings in a phrase, and a phrase may begin either with the first slurred note or, as is more common, with some one of those which precede or which follow it. As a usual thing, phrases and their members are not indicated by a slur or by any other symbol. In the preceding example, where the slurs, as usual, indicate the bowing, were the subdivisions of the phrases also indicated by slurs in the notation there would be another slur cutting across that in the third measure, between *D* and the last *E,* and ending over the *G* in the last measure. These two slurs, articular and sentential, might perhaps appear oppositional in meaning, but this would be merely an appearance, not a reality. Actually, they would no more interfere with each other in function and in application than do the various accents and stresses of rhythm, of melody and of harmony, each of which, governed by its own separate principle, works in essential agreement with that of the others. Bulow wrote of these measures: "A very slight delay on the first half of the third measure, *i.e.,* at the close of the fore-phrase, would not seem inappropriate: for the shorter after-phrase begins, despite the legato slur, only on the fourth beat."

In *Example* 23, taken from the first movement of Beethoven's *Concerto in C major,* the notes have legato slurs, but this does not conflict with additional mental grouping of the notes according to their significance, as indicated by the dotted curves. If this be conceived as a violin passage interpreted by a great artist, the bowing and the subdivisions of the phrasing are readily perceived as being different, yet coexistent.

Example 24

Beethoven — Sonata, Op. 2, No. 3. Allegro.

These few measures from the first movement of the Beethoven *Sonata in C major, Op. 2*, are illustrative of the legato bowing-marks of the composer, combined with dotted-curves which show the mental grouping of the notes according to their sentential significance, into a phrase and phrase-members.

Beethoven.

Example 25

Sonata, Op. 90. Slow movement.

Example 25, taken from the slow movement of the *Sonata in F, Op. 90*, serves both as an illustration of bowing-signs as used by the composer and of phrasing-signs as indicated by the editor. All the slurs and dots over the notes are found in the Beethoven manuscript, and indicate ap-Sentential sub. proximately the desired connection, disconnection divisions. Artkuand attack of tone. (The additional dotted curves lar subdiTision8 outline sentences, phrases and motives, but in so doing convey an almost shockingly mechanical and therefore a false impression of this wonderful melody.) In a number of cases the slur defines both the legato of the notes within its curve and an integral subdivision of a phrase (motive, section, phrase-member). But most of the sentential subdivisions include several small groups of connected notes, of slightly detached notes and of notes very much detached. The legato notes are indicated by slurs, and the various degrees of detachment are indicated by dots over the notes, by notes marked with dots and placed under a slur, and by single notes marked by the absence of these signs. The punctuation of the phrases and of the sentences is not marked by the composer with slurs. Very rarely, indeed, even in elaborately edited publications, is a slur employed to outline these larger sentential divisions. Nevertheless the slur, used to define the phrases, is a symbol very helpful to pupils when added to the score by the pencil of the teacher, as also are additional editorial pencil-markssuggestive of the articulation, of the dynamics, of the melody, of the harmony, of the rhythms, of the tempi and even of the coloring.

As a result of regarding music as a language, it has been deduced that each tone of a phrase is not necessarily sustained significance of until the next tone is heard and that the end of rests a phrase is not necessarily detached from the beginning of the next phrase. There are often rests, both of long and of short duration, within a phrase. Numberless fugal themes, as well as phrases in music of all kinds, include rests. In the works of the masters, rests are replete with significance. It was "by the agitated breathing in the rests" that Schumann, on reading over a newly published opus, recognized the composer to be Chopin.

Example 26

Beethoven — Sonata, Op. 10, No. 1. Allegro.

Phrasing is in part made evident by punctuation, that is, by pauses. These may be extremely slight or very prolonged, and often are not indicated on the printed page. Previous examples are illustrative of sentential pauses. Of rhetorical pauses Schindler writes at length in his "Life of Beethoven." He speaks of Beethoven's "rhetoric," of "the *cesura* which he often employed" and of "the points of repose, where they are not explicitly marked by the composer." Of the preceding example from the *C minor Sonata, Op. 10, No. 1*, he says: "All the written quarter-rests in the higher part are to be augmented by about two, the interrupted phrase being thrown off with vehemence. The aim is to increase the suspense." (Measures 5, 8 and 11 are interpolated.) Example 27 Beethoven— Sonata, Op. 10, No. 1. Allegro.

Of the cadenza before the coda in the first division of this movement he says: "This shows the application of the Beethoven precept; that is, points of repose, where Beethoven's they are not explicitly marked by the composer. ce-suTM These are intended, besides, to mark the dividing line of the coda." The fermatas are added by Schindler.

Example 28

Beethoven — Symphony in C minor. Allegro.

Wagner says apropos of the rhetorical pause over the fourth note of the *C minor Symphony:* "Usually the fermata of the second bar is left after a slight rest; our Beethoven's conductors hardly make use of this *fermata* for fermata anything else than to fix the attention of their men upon the attack of the figure in the third bar. In most cases the *EU,* is not held any longer than a forte produced with a careless stroke of the bow will last upon the stringed instruments. Now, suppose the voice of Beethoven were heard from the grave admonishing a conductor: 'Hold my *fermata* firmly, terribly. I did not write fermatas in jest, or because I was at a loss how to proceed; I indulge in the fullest, the most sustained tone to express emotions in my *Adagio;* and I use this full and firm tone when I want it in a passionate *Allegro* as a rapturous or terrible spasm. Then the very life blood of the tone shall be extracted to the last drop. I arrest the waves of the sea, and the depths shallbe visible; or I stem the clouds, disperse the mist, and show the pure ether and the glorious eye of the sun. For this I put my *fermatas,* sudden, long-sustained notes, in my' *Allegro.* And now look at my clear thematic intention with the sustained *El,* after the three stormy notes, and understand what I mean to say with other such sustained notes in the sequel.'"

The Century Dictionary, discussing the punctuation in use in literary expression, remarks that "long after the use of the close punctua-present punctuation marks became established tion. Open they were so indiscriminately employed that, if punctuation closely followed, they were of ten a hindrance rather than an aid in reading and understanding the text. *Close punctuation,* characterized especially by the use of many commas, was common in English in the eighteenth century, but *open punctuation,* characterized by the avoidance of all pointing not clearly required by the construction, now prevails in the English language. In some cases, as in certain legal papers, title-deeds, etc., punctuation is wholly omitted." The intricate close punctuation which Riemann employs in his editions is of great and permanent interest, even should the reader not agree with his theory that motives never begin upon a strongly accented part of a measure. A greater number of the poems in the English language begin upon an unaccented syllable, but by no means all of them begin in this way.

The principle which has led to the omission of all unnecessary punctuation marks in symbolized speech is peculiarly Beethoven's applicable»to symbolized music. In the preceding declamation paragraph emphasis is laid upon the fact that where the exact meaning of the language is of great importance, punctuation, as on the whole conducive to vital misunderstandings, is wholly omitted. So is it omitted, as a usual thing, in the compositions of the great masters of music. We read that Beethoven "was prevailed upon, after repeated entreaties, to make arrangements for the publication of a complete edition of all his pianoforte sonatas. His determination to undertake this task was influenced by the consideration of three important and, indeed, necessary objects: viz., first, to indicate the poetic ideas which form the groundwork of many of those sonatas, thereby facilitating the comprehension of the music, and determining the style of its performance; secondly, to adapt all his previously published pianoforte compositions to the extended scale of the pianoforte of six and a half octaves; and thirdly, to define the nature of musical declamation (elocution)." But this Beethoven did not do, notwithstanding the fact, indeed perhaps partly because of the fact, that on the topic of musical declamation he went beyond the generally received idea of his day, maintaining that "poetical and musical declamation are subject to the same rules." "Though the poet," he used to say, "carries on his monologue or dialogue in a certain, continuous rhythm, yet the elocutionist ('Declamator'), for the more accurate elucidation of the sense, must make pauses and interruptions at places where the poet could not venture to indicate it by punctuation; and this style of declaiming is

equally applicable to music, and is modified only by the number of persons cooperating in the performance of a musical composition." CHAPTER V
The Acciaccatura-arpeggio

As an acceptable rendition of a musical composition depends primarily upon a correct interpretation of the musical symbolized notation, the performer must be familiar with the speech. Symlanguage of music, both written and audibly boiized music interpreted. If the modes adopted to make the meaning of the music clear to the eye and mind of the reader be not thoroughly comprehended, the player may be as completely mystified as to the composer's idea as a foreigner who for the first time sees words of dissimilar meaning spelled alike, as, for instance, yard *(ground, length);* tale *(story, tally);* seal *(stamp, animal):* or the differently spelled but similarly sounding words tier and tear; air and heir; sent, cent and scent; or those words whose part of speech as well as their meaning is determined by the location of the syllabic accent, as in the words invalid and *invalid;* entrance and *entrance.* These conditions in symbolized speech are akin to those in symbolized music.

The duration of a tone is not indicated with precision and completeness, for neither its beginning nor its ending is always given with absoluteness in the notation. It has

Neither attack.

nor cessation of been demonstrated In a preceding chapter that tone adequately if tne notes of a passage written for the piano be removed from the context the relative duration of the tones represented cannot be definitely indicated by the musical characters representing them. Neither is attack of tone shown with positiveness by the symbols alone.

Example 29 4 6 6 7

Here are eight ways of writing the same manner of playing an arpeggiated chord upon keys so close together that they are easily grasped simultaneously. Yet some of these signs of various signs of arpeggio do not show which tones "peg»o should sound first nor in what order the others should come, nor

whether the chord should be arpeggiated gracefully or stridently. In the case of wide-spread arpeggios written for one hand there are still other means of expressing the same mode of playing, some of which are shown below.

These various forms of notating an arpeggio are in part the outgrowth of a desire to indicate that, although certain notes are so distant from each other that the hand 0rigin o(cannot play them simultaneously, yet the effect acciaccaturaof a simultaneous attack must be attained as arpeggl nearly as possible. Played with this conception of their meaning, these chords may be called *acciaccatura-arpeggios.* The word acciaccatura (pronounced at-cha-ka-tu-ra) is derived from the verb *acciaccare* (to crush). The acciaccatura as found in pianoforte music is of two kinds: first, the acciaccaturaarpeggio, of which all or some of the tones are more or less sustained; second, the acciaccaturagrace-note, which represents an unsustained embellishment tone. A dash across the stem, as in number four of *Example* 29, is the original notation of acciaccatura and is still commonly used across the stem and flag of grace-notes, which are found in vocal and instrumental music of all kinds. The acciaccaturaarpeggio, however, is found only in pianoforte music.

The acciaccatura-arpeggio should sometimes be conceived even when no symbol is used to indicate the character of the chord. Often it is used in imitation of an effect possible only on stringed instruments, upon which, on account of their construction, a solid chord cannot be produced, and so the Arpeggiochord-tones are played rapidly one after another strappata m one D0w and with an equally sudden and force ful quality of attack. An arpeggio thus orchestrally conceived is called an *arpeggio-strappata,* the word strappata coming from a root meaning to wrench or jerk.

Applied to orchestral music, such a manner of playing is called *strappata a"orchestra,* an excellent term for the vigorous strappata harmonic onslaught produced when, on the down d'orchestra Deat of the director, a chord is played fortissimo and very staccato on the stringed instruments, crushing the tones together as just described, while the rest of the instruments also play fortissimo, sforzando and staccato. The final chords of orchestral compositions are often strappata. So are they frequently in pianoforte compositions. This effect should be conceived when playing on the pianoforte such crashing chords as those ending the Beethoven *F minor Sonata, Op.* 57, for the performer will then obtain an orchestral quality of tone which otherwise would be lacking in the rendering.

Example 31

Beethoven — Sonata in F minor, Op. 57. Allegro.

Although intended by the composer to be played in this manner, these final chords are marked in the original by no special sign; but in order to make the manner of performance plainer to the student, Billow in his edition adds staccato dots, *ffz* and *secco.* In other similar cases he also gives explanation of the manner of performance. Very often no sign indicates the necessity for *arpeggio-strappata,* although occasionally signs are employed.

The *Example* at 30 *a* is oftener employed in classic than in modern music, and of all the forms here shown it is the most definite in significance; as it bears the original stroke through sign of *acciaccatura* (a dash across the stem), it is stem, and other undoubtedly an acciaccatura-arpeggio. The no-symbols tation at *d* in the same example, although played in the same way as the three preceding, *a, b, c,* indicates not so much the manner of employing the fingers, as the desired effect — a simultaneousness of attack — which, however, as in all the other cases, from *a* to *i,* is impossible on account of the wideness of the interval to be played. At *e* the same effect is desired — a simultaneous attack of the tones and a sustaining of the basstone; but the impossibility of prolonging the bass-tone by means of the fingers is recognized by writing the bass-note of shorter duration than the other notes of the chord. This is a guide to the mode of execution as far as the

hand is concerned; but the tone must be prolonged beyond its apparent value by means of the pedal.

The connecting vertical slur at / shows clearly to the eye that a simultaneous attack of the tones is wished for, and the use of the slur also recognizes the pianistic impossibility of this. The notes are unavoidably struck one after another, but this should be done so quickly that all the tones sound as though played on the beat. Both Chopin and Grieg frequently employ the vertical slur in this manner. Many instances in point are found in Grieg's own transcription of his *Peer Gynt Suite,* from which the following example is taken.

Example 32

Vertical **Blur**

The notation at 30 *g* is quite indefinite in its significance and is susceptible of several different interpretations. The wavy line wavy line may mean to arpeggiate either grace before chord fully or crushingly and, when used before a chord of several notes, does not indicate the order in which these notes are to be played; the upper note or a middle note may be a note of the melody, which should be struck before the other notes and be given melodic emphasis. Yet it is also often used to indicate an acciaccatura, as is shown in Grieg's own transcription from which the above measures are taken, for later, upon the return of the theme, the chords in the left hand are marked with a wavy line in the same manner as at 30 *g,* instead of with a vertical slur as at the beginning of the movement. In the orchestral score there is no change in the notation upon the return of the theme.

The notation at 30 *h* is frequently employed by editors to show students how the acciaccatura should be played; but, Explanatory although this may give some idea of the necessary notation rapidity of execution, it is perhaps least of all adapted to give a correct idea of the character of the arpeggio, for it does not indicate whether the notes are to be played with grace or vigor, and by the very fact of giving the notes a definite value it makes an incorrect impression.'

The form of arpeggio shown at 30 *i* is

very common in Small notes in-romantic and modern music. The first number dicating use of 0f Schumann's *Davidsbundleridnze* contains similar pedal arpeggios.

Here the bass-note *G,* written of small size, should be sustained by the pedal until it progresses to *C* in the next measure.

The acciaccatura bass-note, 30 *b,* should be more or less sustained. It is not a grace-note, but is written as one merely" because the fingers cannot remain on the key, Theacciaccabut must leap to the other notes of the chord, twabass-note leaving the sustaining of the bass-tone to be accomplished by means of the pedal. *Example* 30 *a* is illustrative of this. The *Example* 30 c is rendered in the same manner as that at *a* and *b,* and is a notation much used by Schumann, not only for bass-notes, but for inner voices of the harmony where the tone must be sustained by the pedal while the fingers jump to a somewhat distant key.

Schumann's notation in the thirteenth and fifteenth measures of the *Farewell* from the *Forest Scenes* is peculiarly interesting for the reason that the bassnotes are written in two ways at the beginning of these measures, first as in the acciaccatura-arpeggio at 30 e, then like that at 30 *b.* Both examples are played in the same manner, as somewhat sustained basstones.

Example 34

Schumann — Forest Scenes, Op. 82, No. 9.

There is no reason for this change of notation except that Schumann may have felt the first notation to be inadequate to express his conception, and so have tried another Schumann's mode of writing the next time he wished to indiquandary cate a necessary release of the key by the finger. However, although the key be released, the tone produced through striking the key should be somewhat sustained by the pedal. Neither the tone of the bass-note at e nor of that at *b* should be short, for neither is an embellishing tone; each is a basstone, the corresponding key of which cannot be held down by the fingers. Of this difficulty in finding adequate notation for a somewhat similar passage in the *Carnival*, Schumann writes in a letter to Moscheles: "You must pardon many things in my manner of setting down the notes. I really did not know how to write the three *A's* above each other.

produces a different effect; the high *A's* should only create a faint lingering echo, and so I could not think of any way to write it but

Examples of these different ways of notating an acciaccatura bass-note are found in many pianoforte compositions. Schumann's *Kreisleriana* contains the following passage illustrative of the various modes of writing the acciaccatura-arpeggio as shown in 30 *b, g,* and *i;* in 33 *i,* and in the example below. Each of the bass-notes, *F, F, B, D, Eb, F,* should be sustained by means of the pedal until it progresses to the next bass-note, but in such a manner as not to blur the melody.

Example 35

Schumann — Kreisleriana, Op. 16, No. 6.

Not only may the bass note be written as grace-note, but so may the notes of any other voice, as at *a* in the following passage from Schumann's *Novelette, in A major.* The t chord. small note, *E,* which easily might be misconceived tone written as as a note embellishing the melody, represents a srace-note chord belonging to the lowest voice played by the right hand, Example 36

Schumann — Novelette, in D Major, Op. 21, No. 8.

and should be sustained as such until it moves to *F,* the next tone of the same voice, as shown in the edited example at *b,* in which the quarter-rest is found where it rightfully belongs, in the middle voice, and the duration of the small note is represented as it actually sounds — sustained, not short. In Chopin's *Berceuse,* many sustained melody notes in measures 15-18 are written as grace-notes.

Example 37

Beethoven—Sonata, in A Major, Op. 2, No. 2. Allegro.

a. Kohler edition. Example 37, taken from the development section of the

first movement of Beethoven's *Sonata, in A major, Op.* 2, *No.* 2, is illustrative of two ways of writing an arpeggiated interval. Kohler's edition of this sonata gives the acciaccaturas *E, F, A,* and Bb in the middle voice as small-sized thirty-second notes, as at a; Klindworth's edition gives them in notes of the usual size placed immediately below the notes to which they are slurred (as in *Example* 30/ and in *Example* 32). In performance both ways of writing are interpreted the same, the middle and lowest voices being strict imitations of the melody in the upper voice. CHAPTER VI

The Acciaccatura-grace-note And Other Embellishments

Among the preceding notational difficulties is that of determining the musical significance of the small note; considerable experience is necessary in order to be able in

A c c i& c c n. 111 r ci stantly to determine its character and duration, arpeggio used Thus far there have been under consideration only only ta P?nosustained acciaccatura chord-tones, and these, whether written as small notes or as large ones, are peculiar to pianoforte music.

The second kind of acciaccatura is common to music of all kinds, and belongs to the class of embellishments. An acciaccatura-grace-note differs from a note of an ac-Acciaccaturaciaccatura-arpeggio in duration, but not in grace-note used character: the one is a sustained chord-tone, the m music other an unsustained ornamenting note played with more or less grace, —hence its name. As a dash across the stem is the original notation of acciaccatura, so an acciaccatura-grace-note is correctly written as a small eighth-note with a dash across stem and flag. The Italians call grace-notes *note senza valore*—notes without value. In classic music, a grace-note is usually struck with all the notes of the chord, excepting the note to which it is slurred and which it embellishes; is played very rapidly and is released when it is connected to its succeeding principal note. Both the principal note and its grace should come on

the beat, so as to maintain the nature of acciaccatura, as explained when discussing acciaccatura-arpeggio, for as the acciaccatura-grace-note is without value of its own, it cannot, of course, appropriate to itself appreciable duration belonging to the note following it. Therefore the commonly used expression, "A grace-note steals time from the note to which it is slurred," is incorrect. Of the thousands of instances which could be cited, the one. given below suffices to show the acciaccatura-grace-note in the two ways in which it occurs. 38 *a* shows the grace-note *BF,* which does not belong to the harmony with which it is struck; at c is shown the grace-note *C,* which is part of the chord with which it is struck. It is easily seen that if this *C* be unsustained it is an acciaccaturagrace-note; if it be sustained, the chord of which it forms part is an acciaccatura-arpeggio. The grace-note in romantic and modern music is often played before the chord.

Example 38

Schubert t — Moments Musicals, Op. 94, No. 3.

Notwithstanding the fact that a chord with a line through its stem was originally meant as an acciaccatura-arpeggio, yet several mean-those musicians are not necessarily wrong who ings of one sign interpret the line across the note *E* in *Example* 39 a to be a sign for an acciaccatura-grace-note, as at *j;* or who would make of the *E* an inverted mordent, as at k, *l,m,n;* for, owing to the prevailing inaccurate use of musical terms and symbols, some composers have employed the dash with these meanings. Besides, much confusion of notation has come about through the mistakes of copyists. Beethoven often complains in letters to his friends and to his publishers that his newly published compositions are "full of blunders and errata. They swarm in them like fish in water, that is, to infinity."

Example 39

Whenever a mordent is employed the significance of its name, which means biting, should be born 3 in mind. The ornamenting grace-notes of this embellishment should often be played bitingly and as fast as possible, although at times they are played with an easy grace. It is the difficulty of notating the effect of several tones sounding on the beat, yet not struck together, that causes editors to indicate the performance of the mordent in different ways when they write it out in small notes. The best editors usually place the accent-mark on the first note, as at 39 *I*, which, on the whole, most nearly suggests the correct performances. Others write it over the third note, as at *m;* and sometimes accent-marks are placed over both of these notes as at *n;* yet each of these notations has the same meaning, and is an attempt, necessarily inadequate, to indicate the correct manner of performance, — all the tones sounding on the beat, yet not attacked together. The Grieg melody at 32 *o* gives an illustration of an inverted mordent written out in small notes.

Sometimes grace-notes, few or many, succeed each other as in *Examples* 32 *p,* 38 *b,* 39, 40, 41 and 44. This class of embellishment, sometimes called a slide, is most Portamento n often written in small notes with connected tails. voce To render it properly, it should be conceived vocally, not pianistically, for it represents an attempt to produce, as nearly as the instrument will permit, the effect known as *portamento di voce* — the carrying of the voice from one tone to another, through the minutest, unwritable, intervening fractions of tones. This is an effect most artistic when properly employed by great singers,— Sembrich is past-master of the art,—but usually should be avoided by students, who often slur their tones because they have not the skill to sing at once, and with pure intonation, the printed notes. Although occasionally indicated in vocal music by the words *portamento di voce* or alluded to in speech by the terms *portando la voce* or *portare la voce,* these words are rarely written down, and the portamento, as usually employed, is a poetic license taken by the artist at his own discretion. The violinist produces a similar effect by rapidly slipping the finger along a string, while producing the tone with the bow,

thus delicately passing through all the nuances of intermediate tones.

Examples of the slide — the pianistic imitation of the The slide portamento — are very numerous in Chopin's

Pianistic porta-music, and emphasize and make clear a part ment0 of his meaning when he said: "You must sing if you wish to play." Example 40 Chopin — Nocturne, Op. 15, No. 2.

If this passage were sung, probably the small notes would not sound distinct in pitch, but would merely form a connecting link of indefinite, unnamable tones, upon which the voice would smoothly glide from *ER* to *A*. In playing this slide upon the pianoforte it should be conceived vocally, and the small notes played with a light, flexible finger-touch. The pedal should be used while playing these notes to connect the principal tones, the more sonorous *Eft* and *At),* without perceptibly blurring the run. Even the very long, pianistic embellishing runs such as occur so often in Chopin's music should each be conceived as ornamenting a single tone, or serving as a gossamer link from one melody tone to another—for instance, in the run from the 5b *Variations* in *Example* 41, where the embellishing notes, originally written of the same size as the principal note, are written by the editor in small notes, as an assistance to the eye in quickly showing the relative expressive ness of the tones. The run should be played with the utmost elasticity of fingers and hand, using pure finger-touch pianissimo, and should sound glissando-like in character.

The chord-note *Al,* may be played with some weight from the forearm and, after a light turn, may be played again with some stress but with a different quality from the first *AF.* It should be sustained by means of the pedal until the chord-note *Dfc* in the next measure is struck, more softly than the *Ah,* but with more tone than the notes of the run. Other Chopin runs used as embellishments are given in *Examples* 96 *b,* 98, 99 and 103. Such passages remind one of Leigh Hunt's description of the playing of Paganini:

"And ever and anon o'er these he'd

throw
Jets of small notes like pearl,...
One chord affecting all."

But romantic music has no monopoly of embellishing runs, for they are quite common in classic music, also. The fifteenth measure in the *E major Adagio* from the Embellishing Haydn *Sonata, in lb* contains a run almost iden-rans tical with that just given in *Example* 41, although in another key, and the runs in measures 21 and 23 are similar in character. These and other passages are so differently notated in the various editions, that a sample passage is here given. The upper staff is copied from the Peters edition, the lower from the Litolff edition.

At *a* the first note is written as a quarter-note, at 6 this is shown as an eighth-note; at *a* the chromatic runs are given in sixteenth-notes, at 6 these same notes are written as sixtyfourth notes; at *a* the *D* below the staff is written as an eighth-note, at *b* this same note appears as an accented sixty-fourth note; at *a* certain notes have above them the staccato dash, at *b* these notes have dots above them. Yet both the notations in the above example have exactly the same significance, the upper one indicating the character of the notes, *senza valore;* the lower attempting to give them an approximate value.

Mozart's music is full of such embellishing passages, an instance of which, taken from the eighteenth measure of the *Rondo, in A minor,* is given in *Example* 43, where all the thirtysecond notes constitute a delicate flourish connecting *A* and *G* (as suggested by the connecting slur).

Embellishments were first introduced in clavier playing as a means of prolonging certain tones of the clavichord and harpsichord, which instruments had little power of sustaining tone. The embellishment notes were given their place in the text inconspicuously; small notes were employed 0 . of as well as symbols representing the trill, the turn pianistic embeiand many embellishments now no longer used. Ushments This we see. exemplified in the music of Bach, Handel, Scarlatti, Rameau, Couperin and other composers of the latter part of the seventeenth and first part of the eighteenth century. The sonority of the pianoforte of today does away with the original necessity for these ornaments, and many of them may be omitted to the advantage of the composition and to a greater preservation of the composer's meaning than if the notation be slavishly adhered to, although a proper use of embellishments often adds greatly to the beauty of a composition. Ph. E. Bach, in his treatise on *The Art of Playing the Clavier,* in which he devotes nine chapters to embellishments, gives warning that although embellishments "serve to connect the tones, to enliven them, and when necessary give them special emphasis," yet their too frequent use must be avoided in order that they may not resemble the ornaments with which the finest building may be overladen or the spices with which the best dish may be spoiled, and he adds that their use is often abused, "for many players imagine that the whole grace and beauty of clavier playing consists in making a turn every moment." "During the last few years my chief endeavor has been to play the clavier, in spite of its deficiency in sustaining sound, as much as possible in a singing manner, and to compose for it accordingly. This is by no means an easy task if we desire not to leave the ear empty, nor to disturb the simplicity of the noble cantabile with too much noise."

As an embellishment is used to ornament a single tone, the first necessity is to ascertain which is the embellished and which are the embellishing tones. All ornament-Vocal concep ing tones should be sung to the same syllable as «on of emtheir principal tone, as was the habit in the time beUishments of the old masters, when singers were musicians who made their art a life-study, and consequently had no difficulty in differentiating the melody from its embellishments. Of course, the fact that ornamenting notes were then written of a smaller size than the main note made it easier than in our notation of today to understand which was the principal note and which were the embellishing notes.

This is one reason why the use of the small note still survives in our notation. It is best to think of all beautifying tones — trills, turns, etc. — as sung in this way, to the syllable of the tone which they ornament.

Example 44

The notes of a trill, like those of all other ornaments, are *note senza valore.* When playing a trill it is essential to know Make-up and which is the chordtone, the only one having rendering of harmonic and rhythmic value, what is the preptnl1 aration of the trill, and what the ending of it.

The hearer should always be more conscious of the principal chord-tone, the one upon which the trill is made, than of the preceding small note (appoggiatura) if there be one. If the trill end with a turn, these final notes should be played with a different touch, more slowly and expressively than the shake in the middle part of the trill, which should be played rapidly and lightly with flexible fingers; all embellishing tones must be delicate, or they have an effect the opposite of ornamentation. Trills are notated in a great many ways. Sometimes the notes are written out in full merely to make the trill easy for the student; but rightly played, the notes of a trill should not be measured. The brilliancy of a trill depends not so much upon its rapidity as upon its evenness and the subdivision of its notes. One means of attaining these is to begin the trill and to finish the turn ending the trill with different fingers from those used for the other notes, as 323, 1323232323, 14323, or some other change of fingering. The trill should be played in such a way as to bring into prominence the principal chord-tone, *a,* which is often the resolving tone of a discord, the note of resolution, *b,* being played more softly, as is usually the case with a discord and its resolution. For this reason, in order not to give undue prominence to the appoggiatura when the trill begins with one, it is sometimes better to play in this manner: beginning slowly, accelerating in the middle and retarding toward the end. First accent the appoggiatura, c, and after a slight shake of a few notes

begin another group of notes, this time accepting the chord-tone, *d,* and subordinating the appoggiatura so as to make of it a changing note. In such a place a singer sometimes swiftly changes the accent from *C* to *B,* aiding the tone-production by shaking her head or even her whole body at the same time. The closing notes of the turn, *e,* should never be hurried, but should be played more slowly and expressively and in such a way as to make satisfactory the resolution of *B,* the embellished tone, to *C,* of the next chord.

Example 46

Bach—Sinfonia from Partita, in C Minor.

When a trill is indicated over a note which is on the same degree as the note last played the embellishment should not be begun with the principal note, but with an Beginning of appoggiatura (see Chapter VII, The Appoggia-*bm* tura), even if not so indicated. Many instances of this kind are to be found in various editions of Bach's music, as in the *Sinfonia* of his *C minor Partita,* where the trill, notated as at *a,* should be played as at *b.*

The turn

Neither should a trill be finished in such a way as to anticipate the note following it. The proper manner of ending a trill is a debated question. Once a number of representative musicians were asked their opinion about this, and their answers varied greatly. Reinecke, the conservative, said that he could never end a trill without a turn. Billow, who though not naturally bold became so through constant association with the greatest musical genius of his day, said that he believed in ending without a turn in passages where there is a succession of trills, as in the Raff *Concerto* and in Beethoven's *Fifth Concerto.* Said Rubinstein: "There are not today two musicians of the same opinion in regard to the rendering of embellishments."

CHAPTER VII

The Appoggiatuba

A small note, when part of an acciaccatura-arpeggio, represents a sustained tone of the melody, of the bass or of an inner voice; as acciaccatura-grace-note, the small origin of note represents an unsustained embellishment *emaU* notes tone. There is still another way in which the small note is employed, especially in old editions; it may be an appoggiatura. Small notes are a relic of the days when our modern notation was in process of making; even as late as the close of the sixteenth century unprepared discords were rare and were written in small notes, as though the composer scarcely dared to give them place in the main text. That great genius Monteverde, by his bold use of unprepared sevenths, had to endure opposition from the musicians of his period, much as did Wagner for his use of distantly related keys and uncadenced, continuous melody, a generation ago. Nowadays this employment of small notes has largely passed away; otherwise we should have more small notes than large ones in our music.

Through mistakes of copyists and engravers, the appoggiatura, when written as a small note, has become confused with the acciaccatura. This is a great error, as Mistakes of the two are as dissimilar as possible in character, copyists True, they look somewhat alike when written of small size and slurred to a following note, but the resemblance is one of notation merely. The two terms became confused when the Renaissance carried Italian music and its terminology to France, Germany and England, where the Italian language was not thoroughly understood.

An appoggiatura is a weighted tone, foreign to the chord with which it is struck, and leans upon a succeeding weaker tone belonging to that chord. As the appoggiatura has definite duration and is dynamically of more importance than

The appoggiatura the t0ne UP011 which *ll* leEI1S' *t* is f C0UrSe a weighted not an embellishment, for this has no durational dissonance value and is played more lightly than the tone to which it forms but a beautifying adjunct.

That this may be made clear to one who has not studied harmony, a simple explanation is given. Two tones which,

consonance when sounded simultaneously, do not incline

Dissonance towards connection with other intervals, but whose relationship is satisfactory and independent, constitute a consonance. All the consonances which can be built up from the note *C* are here given.

These intervals are called perfect unison, *a;* major and minor third, *b, c;* perfect fourth, *d;* perfect fifth, e; major and minor sixth, *l, g;* and perfect octave, *h.* All other intervals which can be built upon *C* are dissonances: these are: all seconds, sevenths and ninths and all diminished and augmented intervals. Similar consonant and dissonant intervals may be made upon any note. Because of their nature to move, dissonances are more provocative of emotion than are the restful consonances to which they progress. A dissonance is normally followed (either immediately or ultimately) by a tone a diatonic half-step (minor second) or a diatonic whole-step (major second) below or above it. This progression of a dissonance to a following tone is called its resolution. "Why trouble to know what a dissonance is?" said the witty Rossini; "it is always a second."

The suspension

If the nature of a dissonance be thoroughly understood, the definition of a suspension is easily grasped. A suspension *(Example 49 b)* is a tone foreign to the harmony which has been prolonged from a tone of a preceding chord, *a.* This tone, before becoming a suspension, and while sounding in the preceding chord, is called the preparation of a suspension, because the harshness of the coming discord is lessened by accustoming the ear to the sound of the tone which is to become dissonant. In order to effect this, the preparation, *a,* should be at least as long as the suspension, *b.* A suspension, if it resolves regularly, moves, like every other dissonance, a diatonic degree to the tone of resolution — the delayed chord-tone, c — the entry of which has been delayed by the suspension. The suspension occurs upon a more accented part of the measure than its resolution.

An appoggiatura is a suspension, pre-

pared or unprepared, and may be of the same duration, *a, b, e, f;* of longer duration, *c;* or of shorter duration, *d,* than the chord-note The to which it resolves. An appoggiatura is usu-appoggiatura ally unprepared, *a, b, c, d,* and is therefore more insistently dissonant than a suspension. If prepared, the appoggiatura is distinguished from a suspension by the fact that it is struck again with the chord. The derivation of the term is from the Italian *appoggiare,* meaning to lean against. Although most frequently but one degree removed from the tone upon which it leans, an appoggiatura may be distant from it any interval (f), omitting entirely the proper tone of resolution, and resolving irregularly, as is sometimes the case in suspensions.

Example 51 *a. Suspension.* f) *Example* 51 a shows an irregular resolution of a suspended *El,* skipping to *AF;* at 6 the *E,* struck with the chord in which The prepared it is dissonant, becomes an appoggiatura. Reappoggiatura garding the rendering of appoggiaturas Ph. Emanuel Bach says: "One can observe that dissonances are generally played stronger and consonances weaker, because the former emphatically fire the passions and the latter soothe them. All appoggiaturas are to be struck more forcibly than the following note." And Sir Francis Bacon refers to "the falling of a discord to a concord, which maketh great sweetness in music."

The appoggiatura should not be termed an embellishment, although unfortunately this is an accepted classification in The appoggiatura most standard dictionaries of music. It is no not an more an embellishment than is a suspension, but embellishment it kas *een* go classed thoughtlessly because it is sometimes written as a small note, and because the word appoggiatura is confused with the word "acciaccatura:" but who thinks of the appoggiatura as an embellishment when it is written as a note of usual size? Yet the manner of notation has, of course, no effect on the character of a musical thought, but is only a more or less successful effort to reproduce this on paper sufficiently well for the executant to recognize the composer's meaning. The acciaccatura may be either dissonant or consonant to the chord with which it sounds; the appoggiatura is always dissonant.

The appoggiatura when unprepared is usually either a half-step or a whole-step above or below the tone to which it resolves, and is correctly written either of the Notation of the same size as this note or as a note of smaller appoggiatura size. In modern music, the appoggiatura is always written as a note of ordinary size. Many recent editions of the classics, also, make no difference between the notation of an appoggiatura and that of any other note. In older editions, while many appoggiaturas are written as notes of ordinary size, others are in the form of small notes, their value — in as far as is indicated by the black or by the hollow head, and by the tails (hooks, flags) on their stems — varying from a half-note to a sixty-fourth-note. Sometimes, though rarely, these appoggiaturas are small dotted-notes. The more common forms in which the small-note appoggiatura is found are the quarternote, the eighth-note, the sixteenth-note and the thirty-secondnote.

In regard to the rendering of the appoggiatura there are several generally accepted rules which often can be followed: (1) Usually, though not invariably, the duration Rendering of the of small-note appoggiaturas is indicated in the appoggiatura same manner as is the duration of a note of ordinary size, by the number of its hooks and its open or black head. (2) The appoggiatura takes half of the value of the tone to which it resolves, if the latter is naturally divisible into two equal parts. (3) An appoggiatura placed before a dotted-note takes twothirds of its value. There are very many exceptions to these rules, which are by no means infallible guides; for the manner of performance of an appoggiatura is largely dependent upon the context. Besides, the rules often conflict with one another. Illustrative of these rules, however, are the small-note appoggiaturas in the first staff in the example below, o, which are played as shown in the second staff, b. The first

note of each of these twelve illustrations is an unprepared suspension.— in other words, is an appoggiatura which should be played with stress.

The confusion of the words "acciaccatura" and "appoggiatura" has given rise to the common mistake of terming the Errors in acciaccatura-grace-note a "short appoggiatura," dictionaries and the appoggiatura itself a "long appoggiatura." It appears to the writer that the usual definitions and explanations of appoggiatura and acciaccatura are manifestly incorrect, in part, though they have the authority of highly accredited reference books. It is strange that even dictionaries by eminent and excellent standard authorities, such as Grove, Elson, Mathews and Liebling, Barrett and Stainer, Hughes, and many others, after correctly defining the appoggiatura and illustrating with suitable examples, yet, following long-established and careless precedents, give sanction to errors, examples of which we quote, italicizing certain words with the object of calling attention to the most glaring mistakes and contradictions. Riemann's Dictionary calls the acciaccatura "an *obsolete ornament* in organ and pianoforte music." Articles in Grove's Dictionary say of the acciaccatura that it is "a now nearly *obsolete* description of ornament, available only on keyed instruments, in which an essential note of a melody is struck at the same moment with the note immediately below it, the latter being instantly released, and the principal note sustained alone. It is generally indicated by a small note with an oblique stroke across the stem, or when used in chords by a line across the chord itself. Its use now is confined to the organ, where it is of great service in giving the effect of an accent, or sforzando, to either single notes or chords. The term 'acciaccatura' is now very generally applied to another *closely allied* form of *ornament, the short appoggiatura."* Of the appoggiatura this dictionary says that it is "One of the most important of *melodic ornaments,* much used in both vocal and instrumental compositions.... The short appoggiatura may belong to the *same* harmony as the principal note, or

it may be *one* degree above or below it. ... With regard to its length, the appoggiatura is of *two kinds,* long and short; the long appoggiatura bears a fixed relation to the length of the principal note, as will be seen presently, but the short one is performed so quickly that the abbreviation of the following note is scarcely perceptible."

From Elson's Dictionary we quote the following: "The principal *embellishments* are the *appoggiatura,* the turn and the shake." He speaks of "the *short grace-note,* or *acciaccatura* or *short appoggiatura* as it is variously called," and remarks that "it will be well to remember that the *long grace-note (appoggiatura)* is yearning and tender in effect, while the short gracenote is bright and crisp, with the single exception of sometimes imitating a sob in mournful or plaintive music." The appoggiatura is defined as *"leaning-note; grace-note,* note of *embellishment.* ... It is one of the most charming embellishments of song and of instrumental music. The cause of writing so long and accented a note as a grace-note lies in the fact that the *appoggiatura* is *almost* always extraneous to the *melody* and to the *harmony.. .. The* appoggiatura is sometimes called the *long grace-note.* Some dictionaries (Grove and others) call the short gracenote 'appoggiatura' also; for the use of the *short appoggiatura* see Acciaccatura. Confusion can here be avoided by using the English equivalents—*Long grace-note* and *Short grace-note."*

Mathews and Liebling's Dictionary says that the acciaccatura is "a species of arpeggio; an accessory note placed before the principal note. Practically *about the same* as an *appoggiatura."* The appoggiatura it calls *"leaning* note, note of *embellishment.* An *accessory* note, or *grace-note,* situated one degree from the principal tone." Hughes remarks that the *acciaccatura* is "a *short appoggiatura,* usually a grace-note, struck at the same time with its principal, but instantly released." Barrett and Stainer's and other well-known dictionaries also make statements similar to the foregoing.

In reference to these quotations but

few words of comment are necessary. The appoggiatura is not a melodic ornament or embellishment, and is not closely allied, nor at all allied, to the acciaccatura. Far from being an ornament, the appoggiatura itself is the principal tone, which is susceptible of ornamentation by other lighter tones. It never belongs to the same harmony with which it is sounded, but is always dissonant. It is oftenest but one degree from its tone of resolution but may be distant from it. The appoggiatura cannot be of two kinds — the character is always similar to that of a suspension. A leaning note is the opposite of a grace-note. The appoggiatura is always extraneous to the harmony, and it is a note of melody in some part, very often that of the main melody. Much confusion is caused by terming notes of two such opposed characteristics as the appoggiatura and the acciaccatura by the similar names of *Long grace-note* and *Short grace-note,* since the appoggiatura is never a grace-note. The acciaccatura is not obsolete, and is not about the same as an appoggiatura, but very different. The appoggiatura is not an accessory note situated one degree from the principal note, but is itself the principal note, requiring resolution.

The first measure of the characteristic Mozart Rondo, which, about forty years ago, was played by Rubinstein on his American tour, is printed in different editions Different ta_ in three ways. In the more recent editions the tions in different appoggiaturas are notated as at *a,* the *G* and *E* editions being of the same size as the following chord-notes *F§* and *D,* to which they resolve; in other publications these appoggiaturas are written as small-note eighths, as at *b,* their duration and rendering being identical with that at *a.* At c the notes are incorrectly written as acciaccaturas.

Example 54

Mozart — Allegro from Sonata, in C major.

Many Mozart editions contain examples of the appoggiatura written correctly and of others written incorrectly. In the above measure from the first movement of one of Mozart's sonatas in C major the small-note appoggiatura *G* at *a,* cor-

rectly written as a thirty-second-note, should be played as one in the manner indicated at *b.*

Example 55

Mozart — Andante from C Major Sonata.

a. Appoggiaturas incorrectly notated
Certain passages in the slow movement from the same sonata are flagrantly wrong in notation. To one who plays incorrect with appreciative taste it is evident that although notation the first *C* in *Example* 55 is a grace-note, the other three, although also written as acciaccaturas, are appoggiaturas and should be written either as at 6 or as at c, and should be uttered expressively.

Example 56

Bach — Loure from French Suite.
a. Notation.
The preservation of the imitations in the different voices in *Example* 56 *a* necessitates the rendering of the appoggiaturas as at *b,* although this breaks Rule 3, given on page 77. This shows that definite rules cannot be laid down, and when attempt is made to do so it is found that the exceptions are almost as numerous as the examples which follow the rule. There are many instances where the meaning of the notation can only be decided upon by a musician of experience; moreover, even-musicians are not always agreed, as can be seen by comparing some of the many editions of almost any Bach composition.

Example 57

Bach — Sarabande from G major Partita.
a. Notation.
The notation of the *Sarabande* in the *G major Partita* contains many small-note appoggiaturas (which in some editions are written as acciaccaturas). In *Example* 57 *a* Dotted.note rethe three small eighth-note appoggiaturas are ceded by small-especially interesting, since, as shown in the note awo«iatara notation of the rendering, *b,* the eighth-notes *G* and *E* represent quarter-notes (notes twice the apparent value as judged from the tails), and the eighth-note *A,* which is struck with them, represents but half their duration—an eighth, as indicated by its tail.

Example 58

Haydn — Sonata, in C# minor.
a. Notation. /fifeftfe *b. Execution.*
In the two preceding measures taken from a Haydn sonata we find several appoggiaturas. At *a* are a small-note C# written as an eighth-note and an E$ written as a small sixteenth-note, also Z)# and *Elf* written of the same size as the *E* and the *F#* to which they resolve. At *b* these are notated as they are played. In the lower staff at *a* is an appoggiatura written as a small-note eighth, which sounds well and is correctly played either as an eighth-note (according to Rule 1) or as a quarter-note (according to Rule 2).

Example 59

Schumann — Bird as Prophet, Op. 82, No. 7.
In some instances a whole composition is founded upon appoggiaturas and their resolutions. Schumann makes such use of appoggiaturas in his *Bird as Prophet* in the *Forest Scenes.* Throughout this piece the appog-made 0f appoggiatura plays an important part, as may be seen & and 7,,, i, M,.A, .xt. their resolutions from the above example, where the dotted eighth- note at a is in each case an appoggiatura, resolving to the following thirty-second-note at *b.*

The Schumann composition may have suggested to Rubinstein his *False-note Etude,* in which the dotted eighth-note of the ascending arpeggiated chord at *a* resolves to the following chord-note at *b.* The first note of each descending arpeggio on the second beat is also an appoggiatura, c. The dotted appoggiaturas D# and C# should sound as though struck on the first beat of the measure, since the preceding tones constitute an *acciaccatura-arpeggio,* the notes of which are written successively. Had the composer so desired, he could have written the notes of the ascending arpeggio one above the other, as indicated at *d* or as at e, which show more distinctly that the long-sustained appoggiatura comes on the first beat.

Example 61

Cramer — Etude, in G major.
Schindler says that "Beethoven gave prominent force to all appoggiaturas,

particularly the minor second, even in running passages." In reference to this Cramer study Beethoven himself says: "Attention must be paid to the accent of the fifth note of each group, which mostly appears as the first note of a minor second. Trochaic measure forms the basis of each group; the first note accented and long, but less so the fifth." Example 62

Wagner — Tristan and Isolde.

The minor second, employed either as appoggiatura or as a tone of a discord, keeps the auditor in suspense until its resolution, the beauty of which is thus enhanced.

That which by itself is unrestful and ugly may be effective, even poetic and beautiful, when placed in its proper setting. "Why rushed the discords in but that harmony

Minor second should be prized?" writes Browning. How we are stirred by the love-motif of *Tristan and Isolde!* Note the expressiveness of the minor seconds:

Example 63 Beethoven — Sonata, in F minor, Op. 57. Allegro assai.

what a profound impression is made upon the feelings when hearing the above measures from Beethoven's *F minor Sonata,* as the thrice-struck Db descends to C! Example 64

Reinecke — Variations, in Eb, Op. 6.

In rapid passages it is sometimes desirable to give special attention to the bringing out of the tone of resolution, which must always be evident to the ear. The above importance of passage from Reinecke's *Variations, in Ely,* for tone of resolution two pianos, will sound very harsh and unpleasing if the performer is not an adept pianist, for the notes played by the thumb of the right hand are apt to sound so strongly as to prevent the auditor from hearing their progression to chord-tones a minor second above. These dissonant tones, although not appoggiaturas, as they occur upon an unaccented part of the measure and resolve upon a more accented part, yet in the rendering should have almost the effect of appoggiaturas — displaced rhythmically.

There is some danger of making over-prominent the appoggiaturas in playing the somewhat similar passages in Buiow's Schumann's *Andante and Variations, in BF,* for amazement two pianos. Great care must be taken to connect the first and third sixteenth-notes of each group to the note of resolution following, and to bring the latter into sufficient melodic prominence; otherwise the rapidity with which the notes are played may give an excess of false-note effect, the harmonic structure becoming vague and the flowing melody distorted. The performer may be a good musician, and yet, through lack of technical skill, be unable to convey the idea to his auditors; indeed, it almost seems as though the very fact of having conceived a piece well sometimes stands in the way of a good rendition, for, having the notes before him, the performer hears with what Schumann calls "the inner ear," and so may neglect to bring to the ears of his hearers that which he himself may feel acutely. Boekelmann records that Billow was requested to play into a phonograph, and "when he came to hear his own performance repeated through the tube, his amazement and horror were boundless. 'That machine isn't worth anything,' he exclaimed. 'It isn't true, I never played like that — never!'"

How To Find A Hidden Melody

When Wagner wrote that "Music is inconceivable without melody" he restated what has been said by all the great composers of the past centuries. In every composi-Melody essential tion, no matter by whom, there must be melody m all muslc or there is no music. This is as true of Bach as of Chopin, of Palestrina as of Liszt. The simplest Clementi or Cramer study should be played musically and so as to present, in some degree at least, the elements of orchestration, audible melody being a prime requisite. But frequently the appearance of the music does not clearly and at once show to the eye the effect desired by the composer; in no case is this more true than in the notation of the melody.

A melody, whether of vocal or of instrumental character, is easily found when it is presented to the eye as Melody hidden a continuous series of notes with separate stems, by fofm of especially if it lies in an outer voice, as in this Chopin nocturne: and it is not hard to recognize when the melody-notes are in the highest voice in a series of solid chords, as in the middle part of the same nocturne.

But very often the location of the melody is not so immediately evident; it may lie in the upper voice of arpeggiated Melody in upper chords, and, perhaps, upon unaccented parts of voice of broken the measure, as in Cramer's *Study, in A minor,* '""'"' 68 *a,* where the notes of the right hand, apparently constituting one voice, really belong to three voices.

In the majority of cases where the melody lies among the notes of arpeggiated chords, *a,* it can be found most readily and certainly by playing the notes of each group as a solid chord, as at *b,* so that the progression of the harmonies voices may be heard plainly. In this case the «,ta?ed a!» melody is at once felt to be in the soprano. A search for these notes of melody in the original notation at *a* shows each one to be the second of a group of thirty-secondnotes, as at *c,* where the tenuto-mark and the large-sized notes with added upturned stems of the value of an eighth serve to indicate with prominence the melody-notes and the cantabile touch with which they should be played — a touch very different in quality from that of the other voices; for even studies in technic should not be rendered mechanically, the notes and nothing more, but should be made also studies in expression.

d. Six ways of symbolizing melodic stress. 1) 2) 3) 4i 5 6)

As a rule the composer chooses the easiest means of transcribing his thought, as is the case in 68 a; but the melody notes might have been written in either of several other ways, as shown in these six different notations, *d,* of the first group of thirty-second-notes, where, in order that the melody-note may be more readily perceived, it is written at 2 with added stem, at 3 as a large-sized note, and at 4, 5 and 6 is pointed out by having placed above it an accent-mark, a dot, a tenuto-mark. A combination of these or other symbols might have been employed by the composer had he so desired. One such combination is given in the edited notation at c.

According to the eminent London musical critic, J. S. Shedlock, Beethoven, despite his dislike of teaching, personally See "Selection of Studies by J. B. Cramer, with comments by L. van Beethoven, and preface, translation, explanatory notes, and fingering by J. S. Shedlock, B.A." Published by Augener & Co., London, 1893.

annotated for the use of his beloved nephew, Karl, twenty-one of Cramer's studies, deeming them the best preparation toward a correct interpretation of his own pianoforte

Beethoven's.

annotations to compositions. Beethoven says of the above *Study,* Cramer's *n A minor:* "The melody throughout lies in the **Etudes** second note of each group. This study should be given at first in very moderate tempo and with pretty strong, though not short, blows. In proportion as the tempo is afterward increased the sharp blows will decrease, and the melody and character of the study will stand out in a clearer light. " He also calls attention to the fact that a passage may be written in more than one way, as in this study:

Example 69 of which he says: "The movement is written throughout in four voices. The melody lies in the upper voice, as is shown by the mode of writing. Were, however, the latter as follows: *b . v v .?*

still the first note of each group would have to be uniformly accented and held down. The middle voice-notes *g c, f c, g c,* etc., must not be given out with the same strength as that of the upper voice. The measure shows itself as trochaic."

Example 70

In regard to the above *Study, in D minor,* he says: "In the first five measures the first note of the first triplet and the third note of the second triplet must be connected together in the best possible manner, so that the melody may stand out thus: -f». — —ja

The finger, therefore, must remain on

the long note."

Example 71

Of this 6tude Beethoven says: "The first note of each group bears the melody in closest connection; hence the finger ought not to leave the key until the next melody-note is connection of struck. Only thus will proper connection be melodic tones achieved." In reference to other studies he says: "The triplets constitute a melody-bearing figure." "The melody, which is unequally distributed, must be brought out." "Strict connection throughout." "The intelligence of the pupil becoming gradually more formed will help and proper connection will be obtained." "By paying heed... the melodic movement stands out in passages; without so doing every passage loses its meaning." The burden of all his remarks is that all tones should be suitably sustained, connected and given proper dynamic force while at the same time preserving the natural measure-accents.

Let us find the melody in the arpeggiated chords of this beautiful little piece, 72 *a.*

Example 72

Bach — Prelude, in C minor.

a. Bach's notation. (3 measures.)

A Bach melody

It appears to the eye as a dry, uninteresting finger-exercise, yet it is truly great in its wonderful harmonies and expressive melody. Where is the melody? For there is always melody, no matter how little it moves. Played in the same way as the *Cramer Study, in A minor,* with all the tones of the harmony sounding simultaneously, the first few measures of the piece sound as at *b,* and we hear in each measure but one melodic tone, which in the original notation is the last note of the first beat of each measure, as shown at c.

The first prelude in Bach's *Well-tempered Clavichord,* similar in character to this, also resembles it in form *a.*

Example 73 Bach — Prelude, in C major, Well-tempered Clavichord, *a. Notation. (2% measures.)*

Here also there is but one note of melody in each measure. How simple, yet how beautiful is this melody! how

rich these chords! This surely is religion expressed in music. Qne note. In order to awaken the right conception of the melody in each composition as a whole and to gain a full enjoy-measure ment of its melodic and harmonic beauties, as well as a perception of the contrapuntal progression of the five voices, the entire piece should be played in the same manner as the others, in unbroken chords, as at *b.* In this piece the notes of the melody occur on the second beat of each measure, and should be played so as to give the required character to the tone; for one should aim, as Bach says in the preface to his *Inventions,* "above all, to acquire a cantabile style of playing."

After playing these pieces thoughtfully, first in solid chords, then as intended by the composer, it becomes ,,, ,, . Melodic stress an easy matter to find and to bring out the melody at *a* in the following excerpt from Schubert's *Moments Musicals, in C# minor.*

Example 74

Schubert — Moments Musicals, C# minor.

a. Notation.

When the harmonies are played in chords as at *b,* the melody is heard in the upper voice. Therefore the last sixteenth-note of each group should be played with the required melodic emphasis as shown by the larger notes and added tenuto-marks at c. Such a manner of playing in unbroken chords or intervals is a good study in a simultaneous use of various qualities of tone, which qualities should be imitated when playing the piece in its arpeggiated form. Of course, the melodic stress does not displace nor weaken the grammatical or rhetorical accents in this or other pieces. si Example 75

a. Schubert — Impromptu, Op. 90, No. 4.

Sometimes, as in this Schubert *Impromptu, a,* the melody lies in the highest voice of chords alternately arpeggiated and solid. Students frequently play the chords in measures 5 and 6 in a dragging manner and as though there were no connection in spirit between them and the measures preceding and succeeding.

If the first part of the *Impromptu* be played through in chords as suggested at *b* the melody is at once perceived to belong to the highest voice both of the arpeggiated and of the solid chords. This manner of playing likewise assists the ear to a more ready appreciation and enjoyment of the harmonies. Similar cases of melody hidden in arpeggiated harmonies are very numerous. Such passages are found in Beethoven's *Sonata in F minor, Op.* 57 (see *Example* 9), in the *Andante* of his *G major Sonata, Op.* 14, *No. 2*, in his *Variations on a Theme by Righini*, and in his *Variations on a Russian Theme*. Too often the melody in arpeggiated harmonies remains hidden from the player; how often one hears Chopin's *Etude, in C major* uncomprehendingly played — with brilliancy, perhaps, but nothing more. But what life, what shimmering melodies de Pachmann brings to our ears when he plays it!

The melody may come "unequally distributed" upon both unaccented and accented parts of the measure, as in Liszt's transcription of Schubert's *Gretchen at the Spinning-Wheel*.

In all of these instances the difficulty in finding the melodynotes is twofold: they are concealed by the arpeggiated form, of the chord and also because they occur upon the su ht rhythmic less accented parts of the measure. Yet it is not value of extremely difficult to discover; for when the melodlc tones chords are played in solid form the melody is heard to lie in an outer and therefore a naturally prominent voice; it should be played with no less distinctness when found in an inner voice, as in this arrangement of Schumann's *At the Fountain*.

Instead of simplifying the notation, the double stems in the upper staff at *a* are rather a source of confusion in so far as Melody in an finding the melody is concerned, because in the inner voice frst measure the lower stems are attached to notes of the melody and in the next measure to accompanying notes. In the second measure the upper stems belong alternately to notes of the melody and to the accompanying Fit in the so-

prano. Played in chords it becomes clear that only one voice moves melodiously — that given at *b*.

Example 78 Saint-saens — Toccata, F# minor, o. *Notation.*

Another example of melody in an inner voice is given at 78 *a*, where the upper two notes in the right hand constitute accompanying harmony which flows as shown in the large notes at *b*, where a full harmony is written upon the accented beats of each measure.

Contrasting with these examples is that at 10, and the themes of the Bach *Fugues in C# major*, from Part I, and *G major*, from Part II, of the *Well-tempered Clavichord*, for while an arpeggiated harmony of several notes often contains but one melodic tone, this is by no means always the case, since, as these examples show, successive notes belonging to one harmony may all be melody notes.

Example 79

Bach — Allemande, from Partita, in A minor.

a. Original notation.

The above from the *A minor Partita* gives the notes played by the right hand. At *b* the large notes give the principal melody, made both of the scale and of arpeggiated Melody accom. harmonies interspersed with passing notes, and panied by self-having frequent wide skips down and up; while madehannony occasionally other voices of the same pitch as the melodic tones and entering with them, form sustained and accompanying har monies (in small notes) above the melody. In the original notation, *a;* this is not quickly evident to the eye, as all the notes are of the same size. *Examples* 80, 81 and 82 contain similar manifestations of the same principle.

Example 80

Bach—Prelude, in F major, Well-tempered Clavichord, Part II.

a. Original notation.

The main theme in the *Prelude, in F major* is even more involved in appearance, although immediately evident to the experienced musician. The edited notation at panied themat-*b* shows the main melody written in large notes, icaiiyand and a close scrutiny of the oth-

er parts makes it clear that this melody is accompanied both thematically and harmonically.

Example 81

Schumann — Kreisleriana, Op. 16, No. 1.

a. Original notation.

It is often difficult to disentangle the melody from the accompaniment when the notation includes directions concerning the execution, as in these notes from the *Kreis*-simple notation *leriana, a,* which represent, not one, but five voices, o£ fiTe voices as is seen when the notes are written in chord form on two staves at *b*. Schumann chose the simplest notation; and he assumes his interpreter to be a thorough musician for whom it is unnecessary to indicate the melody more clearly. Had a prominent notation of the melody seemed to him of paramount importance, he could have written the passage in either of several other ways, for instance as at *c*.

The main melodic voice may cross other voices once or many times, so that it appears as the highest note in one harmony, the lowest in another and in a middle voice of still another harmony. Besides which, the notes of the accompaniment and those of the melody may be divided be

Melody played . by right hand tween the right and the left hand, in a manner and left hand grs empl0yeci by Schumann, of which a good in alternately f /,. _ , , stance is found in *Example* 2, and the melody may not be immediately evident to the eye, for the highest voice may be given added stems by the composer for harmonic reasons, not, as is often the case, to assist the eye in finding the notes of the melody.

Sometimes the melody, duet-like, alternates between voices. Often it is interwoven with other voices, as in variations of comMelody sounding plicated pattern, although in that case the original through rests theme helps in finding the melodic tones. It may be difficult to distinguish the melody from its embellishments, as in *Example* 95 *a*. Not infrequently some of the melody notes should be prolonged through rests written for the fingers and not for the tone, as in *Example* 113 and in this *Etude* by Chopin.

Example 82

Chopin — Etude, Op. 10, No. 8, F major.

a. Notation.

This melody is sustained by means of the pedal and the fingers. The *C* on the third beat of the first and third measures should be played very softly so as not to disturb the sustained effect of the *C* of the first beat, which should sound until the *C* on the fourth beat is produced. The melody sustained and connected in this way flows naturally and expressively as Chopin intended, and sounds as at *b.*

These few examples, types of but few of the many ways in which a melody may be hidden by the form of its notation, give some idea of the manner in which notes of the melody may be sought, and the pianist with musicianly insight and experience will successfully solve all problems of this nature which continually confront him in both classic and romantic music. When found, the notes of the melody must be played with suitable quality and duration of tone, for, as Beethoven says, without melody every passage loses its meaning.

CHAPTER IX

Harmony: Duration And Dynamics Of Tones In The Different Voices.

In an analysis of the harmonic structure of a composition each chord receives manifold consideration in order to bring out correctly its various lights and shades,

"Untwisting all the chains that tie
The hidden soul of harmony."

First, each harmony may be thought of as an isolated entity composed of notes whose tonal relation to each other must be felt both by player and by auditor. Some of these tones are more instrumental than others in giving individuality to a harmony, and the interval for which it is named usually may be considered as most characteristic.

Example 83

Characteristic tone of a triad

In the minor triad, *b,* and in the major triad, *c,* the characteristic interval is the third; in the diminished triad, *a,* and in the augmented triad, *d,* the fifth is the distinctive interval.

Example 84

In playing any chord of the seventh, *a, b, c, d,* whether diminished, minor or major, the seventh is the most strongly emphasized tone of the chord if this be unassociated with other chords; but the diminished minor, major, and augmented triads, *a, b, c, d,* upon which chords of the seventh are built, retain also their characteristic intervals, whose comparative stress should be brought out with different qualities of touch. For instance, if the chord of the seventh is built upon the dominant, c, the third is as expressive in its own way as the seventh. In a chord of the ninth, , the dissonant ninth, whether major or minor, is of greater harmonic interest than the other chord tones, although each of these keeps its individuality.

The notes of any chord may be played with such variety of touches that, although the harmony remains unaltered, its import varies; for with change in tone-color variations in come new meaning and different feeling. This is chord-color exemplified in the following ten illustrations in *Example* 85 /, 9, *h.*

At / a chord of the diminished seventh is given three times, the large note in each chord suggesting emphasis of the tone it represents, while the small notes are intended to be played more softly, as accompanying tones. In playing each chord at *g* two of the notes may be given greater stress than the two others which are written small; at *h* one note only is intended to be softly played while the other three are given greater prominence — each with its individual quality of tone different from that of the others. It is apparent that the possible combinations of tone qualities in one chord only are innumerable, since any one of these tones may be played with very many different qualities and each may be combined with the others, all of which also may be played with any one of a variety of qualities.

But as a chord does not occur in music isolated from all others, let us find the main characteristic tones of the triads given in *Example* 83, when they are considered in couples, and horizontally.

As a color when brought into contrast with one brighter seems dull by comparison, and when compared with one more Melodic lines in somber than itself appears to be of brilliant hue, chord-connection so the color effect of a chord varies with its surroundings, the character and strength of each tone depending much upon the nature of the chords with which it is connected. A comparison of the diminished triad, *a,* with the minor triad, *b,* shows that of the three notes constituting each chord the fundamental and the third are common to both; the distinguishing tones in the connection of these two triads are therefore the tones remaining, the fifth of each triad, which may be played with rather more tone than the other notes. But if the minor triad, *b,* is conceived of in connection with the major triad, c, the third of each chord is seen to be the only tone not common to both chords; and as *El,* and *E* are the tones which differentiate these two harmonies they should be given tonal prominence. If the connection is that of a major triad, c, with an augmented triad, d, the distinguishing tone is the fifth, and the melodic succession G to G# should be brought into greater notice than the repeated tones *C* and *E.* The large notes indicate the characteristic tones which form the moving and consequently the interesting voice in each of these three illustrations. In the connection of each two chords grouped together between bars, at 84 *a, b,* c, d, e, it is evident that the moving voice is of melodic as well as harmonic interest, although, as each illustration stops with an upward progression of the unresolved seventh, it is rather displeasing to the ear. Discords, "dear to the musician," are finally followed by concords, and in such a connection of chords each dissonance usually should be given more stress than the interval to which it resolves, as in *Example* 49, and as shown in the following example, where *a* is the dissonance and *b* the resolution.

'The melodic interest of voices accompanying the principal melody should be given due observance. No matter how the music be notated, the player should feel and make Contrapuntal his auditor feel this contrapuntal progression of progression of the voices as they pass through the different har-vol-ces monies, each voice bearing a sub-melody of more or less beauty. Says Hauptmann: "The chief aim of the music we are discussing is harmony, but if it be worth anything, it must be determined by the melody of the several parts." Sometimes the tones of these auxiliary melodies are so soft as scarcely to be heard; at other times they assume a prominence second only to that of the main melody; and occasionally, for variety, one of them may even for a short time usurp the supremacy.

A case in point is Rubinstein's manner of playing Chopin's *Ballade, in Ab,* in which, at the reappearance of the theme in the highest voice, *a,* he brought out most prominently secondary the tenor, here given in large notes, *b,* which at the melody first time of playing was heard merely as an accompanying voice. This way of playing the passage has since been adopted by most players. Both in tenor and in soprano each melodic tone is sustained and connected to the next, regardless of the fact that all are written as eighth-notes.

Example 89

Chopin — Nocturne, in F# minor, Op. 55.

a. Original notation.

The above extract at *a* is copied from Klindworth's edition of Chopin's *F minor Nocturne, Op. 55.* The parts played by the Harmony made left hand have harmonic interest and the triplets of melodies m the right hand represent two beautiful melodies moving in contrary motion. A complete notation of the exact duration of the tones is undesirable,- for it obscures the rhythmic formation and makes the passage hard to read; it is so written at *b,* where the slurs and the direction of the stems help to show the melodic formation. The connection of tone in these two melodious voices is obtained entirely with the fingers, which must be possessed of a developed

and refined control of tone, and of skill in shifting on a key and in sliding from one key to another without making a break in the legato, as is shown in *Example* 125. The bass is held at first by the fingers, and then by the pedal, which should not be used as indicated by the pedal-marks at *a,* which, as so often happens, even in good editions, are incorrectly placed. (See *Examples* 119-121.)

Example 90

Beethoven — Sonata, in D major, Op. 10, No. 3. Presto. Closing measures; theme in augmentation.

a. Original notation.

Bass voice

The bass voice usually lies in the lowest note of each chord and is always of great importance as the foundation upon which rests the whole superstructure. The bass is often melodically significant; and if it have thematic import, it should be rendered so effectively that "it will discourse most eloquent music."

The above example is taken from the close of the first movement of Beethoven's *Sonata, in D major, Op. 10.* A comparison of this *a* with measures 7 and 8 of the theme at the beginning of the movement *b* shows that, combined with an inverted organpoint upon the note *D,* there is an arpeggiated progression in thirds corresponding in harmonies to the thirds at *b.* This thematic imitation must be made obvious to the ear, and especially in the bass voice, which, as shown at c, carries the theme in augmentation and on strong beats of the measure. This is evident in the harmonic structure at *d.* Example 91 Cramer — Etude, in E minor.

Beethoven, in his annotations of the Cramer studies, speaks not only of the treatment of the melody but also of sustaining Beethoven's certain tones of the harmony, even when not so directions indicated in the notation. Of this one in E minor he says: "The rhythmic accent must be uniformly placed on the first note of each triplet. In the four introductory measures, the thumb adheres firmly to the fundamental note, so that the broken triads, and, in a similar manner, all broken chords, may be made clear.

In order to obtain connection (of tone) the triplet figure in the left hand must be dealt with in the same way." Such a sustaining of tone is here indicated by the insertion of dotted half-notes.

In regard to this *Study, in G minor* Beethoven gives the direction that "On account of the connection the first note must always be held on." Such remarks are merely outlines suggestive of correct performance, which Beethoven probably elaborated in his verbal teaching, for they are but meager indications of the way in which he himself played such passages. In common with his predecessors, Beethoven used an expressive accentuation and emphasis combined with a deft prolongation of certain tones much more freely than the few examples annotated for a comparative beginner in pianoforte playing might seem to indicate. Schindler, in his Biography, speaks of Beethoven's "manner of holding particular notes, which, combined with a kind of soft, gliding touch, imparted such a vivid coloring."... "It was more especially the rhythmic accent which he generally desired to have strongly brought out. On the other hand, he usually treated the melodic accent as the situation required, only being in the habit of accepting all suspensions, particularly that of the minor second in cantabile, more emphatically than other players whom we had heard. This imbued his playing with a characteristic pregnancy quite different from the smooth, shallow performances which never reach the height of tonespeech."

The tones of a harmony when produced successively do not form a chord; neither do they make a melody, since they do not succeed each other in a melodic line, but overlap Legatissim0j each other. In consequence, the tones of such a superiegato, harmony are called arpeggiated, because, like annomoso tones successively produced on a harp *(arpa),* they continue sounding together, although produced one after another. The word "arpeggio," therefore, might be preferable to the term "broken-chord," which is often used in reference to such arpeggiated harmonies as those in *Examples* 9 and 68-75. Czerny speaks of this overlapping of tones of the harmony as "legatissimo." Moscheles, Liszt, von Billow and other musicians also use this word, but the more correct term "superlegato" is preferable, since legatissimo merely means very legato, while the word superlegato means over-legato (more than legato), the continuing of a tone for more than its written duration, and after a following tone of the harmony has been produced. Instead of discontinuing the tone as soon as its connection (legato) is made with the tone following, it is prolonged beyond the point of legato and becomes superlegato. The word "armonioso," derived from the same root as the word harmony, also indicates this superlegato manner of playing. In modern editions of the classics, such as the Bach-Busoni, the BeethovenBulow, the Schubert-Liszt and the Chopin-Klindworth editions, superlegato effects, as conceived by the composer, are often more fully indicated by the editors. Superlegato of a few notes or of one note only is sometimes desired; although very often, when by added stems or other signs the editor indicates its use for a few notes only, it is because the necessity for superlegato is greater for these than for others, and, as has been demonstrated in many examples, notably in *Example* 1 and in many examples of Chapter VIII, because even when a complete writing out of a necessary superlegato is possible it is often undesirable.

Example 93
Notes of arpeggiated harmonies are usually sustained for more than their written value, by the fingers, by the pedal, or by both. In the time of Bach a superlegato playing of an undulating arpeggio was often indicated under solid chords, as in his Chromatic Fantasie, of which a couple of measures are given at 93 a. These chords represent the first of a series of arArpeggio. peggios of which the first, written out in arpeggio

Arpeggio legato form, (1), is followed by solid chords, (2), intended by Bach to be played in the same arpeggiated manner, as indicated by the word *arpeggio* written beneath them. This no-

tation is in accordance with that of the authoritative Bach Gesellschaft edition, an edition which gives the text as it is in the original manuscript, and, in cases where the original manuscript is no longer extant, makes use of the oldest copy by Bach's pupils, or the oldest published edition. Many of the old editions employ the words *arpeggio legato* in place of the word *arpeggio* in this composition, as do also some of the more recent editions. Many instances of this manner of indicating an undulating and sustained arpeggio are found in the original editions of Handel's clavier works, for this way of writing was also adopted by harpsichordists. The same effect was called for by the use of a vertical slur placed before a chord connecting the lowest and the highest notes; however, this manner of playing was much more frequently employed than indicated, and very few composers of the time, with the exception of Couperin, took the trouble to indicate so exactly this necessary prolongation of tones.

In more recent editions the execution of these arpeggiated chords is more fully indicated, as at *b,* where the use of the pedal causes each arpeggiated tone to overlap its successors and to sound until the pedal is released when beginning to play the next arpeggio, although even then the fingers, and later a renewed pressure of the pedal, continue to hold the melody and certain other tones until they are connected to those in the next arpeggio. Were the execution of only the first arpeggio written out in full as it sounds, it would have the complicated appearance shown at c, where the large notes are used to point out the attacked tones. Billow's edition more fully indicates the superlegato and gives the bass in octaves to make the passage more sonorous. In reference to this passage Mendelssohn wrote: "I take the liberty to play the arpeggios with every possible *crescendo* and *piano* and *ff.,* with pedal as a matter of course, and the bass notes doubled as well.... N.B. Each chord is broken *twice,* and later on only once, as it happens." *Example* 93 *e* gives these arpeggios as played by Men-

delssohn.

The measures in 94 *a* are taken from the popular Henselt *Etude.* The signs *Fed.* and *0,* although incorrectly placed (see *Examples* 119-121), indicate that the stac-Leatomelod cato basses should be sustained. The staccato is superiegato for the fingers, not for the tone. (See *Examples* harmonies 89, 114, 116.) Superlegato touch is called for by the more customary word "legatissimo," and the stems pointing alternately up and down indicate an alternate use of the hands. At *b* the notes of the melody are written large, the notes of the bass are given approximately their durational value, and a desirable, though slight, arpeggiating of the chords is indicated by the usual wavy line. The necessary superlegato of all the arpeggiated tones of each full harmony is briefly called for by the word *Ped.* at the beginning of the composition. Signs denoting an exact use of the pedal would make a very complicated notation, but the melody must be legato, each note of it must be clearly connected to the next, without blurring the passing tones and the appoggiaturas in sixths, or making a superlegato of the melody-notes belonging to the same harmony. But notes of the harmony, here written small, must be played superlegato. At C, the melody is in large notes, and important harmonic tones, which are attacked at the same time as the melodic tones, are represented in small notes. All the arpeggiated notes which are omitted at c, should be played more lightly, as they merely fill in the superlegato harmony. All the examples at *a,* in the original edition from 74 to 79, should be played superlegato, so as to obtain correct harmony with each melodic tone and to sustain the bass tones.

By employing a varied accentuation and a greater or less prolongation of certain tones, the pianist whose fingers have attained absolute independence of each other will so adjust the relative values of each harmony as to make most prominent those tones of a harmony which, considering its environment, are most needed to bring out its essential traits, to make evident the contrapuntal flow, and to support the melody. To a certain extent these tones can be found by any one who has a musical and hearing ear, even if he has no knowledge of theory, by playing the harmonies in unbroken form. He can experiment as shown in *Examples* 85 and 87, giving the more force now to this tone, and now to that, until the most expressive and best balanced combination of light and shade is found. The musician-pianist, however, intuitively, and without experiment, feels which are the more characteristic progressions.

The problem of a correct treatment of the harmony is a complex one. To play with such ease that the performer's mind is not distracted from the music by the Themodern thought of the means used to interpret it, requires pianoforte, a ready technic and experience in using it to the odern tec c best advantage. In playing upon the sonorous pianoforte of today, and especially upon the instruments of this country, with their deep drop of key and heavy action, much skill is necessary to bring out the meaning of a composition. But a technic sufficient to produce, by variety of touches, the distinctive quality, quantity and duration of tone, combined with musical understanding, insures correct performance. In every composition that he may play the interpreter should make application of his theoretical knowledge, so that the auditor may enjoy a well-phrased melody upheld by interesting progressions of each accompanying voice and by sufficiently sustained harmonies founded on a correct and expressive bass. Says Schumann: "Melody may be compared to chess: the queen, viz., melody, has supreme power, but the final issue rests with the king, viz., harmony." CHAPTER X

A Theme Of Chopin Interpreted

"Ah, my friend, why do you take this piano composer for a weakling? Why give him over to the tough mercies of the Musical prepa-Young Person?" protests Mr. Huneker, in his ration for illuminating and brilliant essay, *The Greater* chopm-piaymg *Chopin.* It is unfortunately true that Chopinplaying is usually begun far too soon, and while

the student is immature not only emotionally but musically, intellectually, and technically. A high order of talent and of equipment is necessary to the interpretation of Chopin's works. Extensive preparatory study of Romantic music, as exemplified in the etudes and pieces of Heller, Jensen, Haberbier, Henselt, Field, Mendelssohn, Grieg, Raff, Rubinstein, and other composers, is indispensable. For until the player has entered fully into the spirit of romance in general, the individual characteristics of Chopin's poetic works cannot be revealed to him; he has no idea of the esthetic content, and does not even perceive the musical meaning of the notes. Ignorant not only of the language in which the music is written, but of its very alphabet, it is in vain for him, conceptionless, to attempt an interpretation. The player should have become thoroughly acquainted with much classic music of all styles; he should enjoy the beauty of Mozart and take pleasure in the simplicity of Haydn; he should be imbued with a love of Beethoven's orchestrally conceived piano music, and delight in the songful Schubert; above all, he should be, as was Chopin himself, a devotee of Bach, the master of masters.

Complete appreciation of the exquisite formal perfection of Chopin's music calls for a theoretical knowledge sufficient to enable the student to compose correctly in the various musical forms. He must have full and instant command of touch, so that if necessary the ten fingers may simultaneously produce ten different degrees of tonal force, Technical quality, and duration. Sonority, delicacy, volu-equipment bility of tone; strength, accuracy, and speed in necessai7 touch, and nicety in pedal control are all prerequisites to the playing of Chopin's music.

Poetic temperament cannot be taught — one has it or has it not; a musical and hearing ear can only be acquired through the continued and critical use of that organ; and finger dexterity comes only through well-directed and assiduous practice. But the structure of a piece and an intelligent understanding of its

notation can in some small measure be learned through the written word, and the object of this chapter is to give a partial analysis of a few measures of Chopin's Bb *minor Nocturne,* practically applying and elaborating the suggestions given in the preceding chapters.

Chopin's first Nocturne, *Op.* 9, written when the composer was only twenty-three years old, is among the simpler and more easily comprehended of his compositions. A com-comparison of parison of editions will be found most helpful, editions Klindworth's edition breathes the Chopin spirit, and the annotations in the Kullak edition are especially helpful in stimulating the imagination. An edition in accordance with the original should also be consulted, that the student, by comparing its notation with that of the above mentioned and other editions, may become aware of different musicians' conceptions of the composer's meaning, and gradually become able to form his own conception and make his own edition. For, of course, Chopin, in common with all writers, expresses by signs but few directions as to the " declamation." In a degree, this is true of speech-writing, where the words and signs are intended for but one performer; how much more is it the case in music-writing for the pianoforte, where notes and signs may represent the simultaneous declamation of many voices!

Liszt, in his *Life of Chopin,* writes: "As the manifold forms of art are but different incantations, charged with electricity from the soul of the artist, and destined to evoke the latent emotions and passions in order to render them sensible, intelligent, and, in some degree, tangible; so genius may be maniEmbeiiishment fested in the invention of new forms.... In arts forms m which sensation is linked to emotion, without the intermediate assistance of thought and reflection, the mere introduction of unaccustomed forms, of unused modes, must present an obstacle to the immediate comprehension of any very original composition." Throughout this Nocturne the student is brought face to face with "unaccustomed forms" of embellishment which are peculiarly Chopinesque.

Example 95 *a*

Chopin — Nocturne, in Bb minor, Op. 9, No. 1.

a. Mikuli edition.

The two-measure phrase consisting of sixteen notes, with which the melody begins, is given in various guise no less than six times, beginning, respectively, on the second half of the measures 1, 3, 9, 11, 71, and 73. In measures 1, 2, and 3 the principal thematic phrase makes its first appearance as follows: Example 96

a. First Thematic Phrase.

Immediately upon the close of this two-measure thematic phrase it reenters in the second half of the third measure with intricate ornamentation.

b. First variant of the above. Original notation.

Thematic value of certain notes

The many embellishing notes and the melodic notes are all written as eighths with connected stems, for they are intended to sound perfectly even; the number of notes grouped together is indicated by the figures 11 and 22. At first sight these notes may seem to have but slight connection with the opening theme which immediately precedes them, but a close analysis shows them to be nearly related. This can be demonstrated advantageously by analyzing each measure separately.

In order to make clear to the beginner in Chopin-playing the relative thematic values of these notes and of the notes of the other variants of the first and second measures of the melody, they are written in the following two examples under the opening melodic phrase from which they are derived, that their parentage may be readily discovered. The figures under the key-signature indicate the measures from which the notes are taken. (For the more intelligent understanding of this analysis, see examples 95 *a* and *b* as well as the shorter extracts.) Large notes are here used to denote the melody, while small notes embody the embellishment thrown round it. Ordinarily the size of the notes is uniform throughout a composition, although Billow in his edition of the *Etudes* often indicates tones of especial expressiveness by the use of two different sizes of notes. Chopin himself has but once employed this means of making the melody notes prominent—— in his AF *major Etude, Op.* 25; but this manner of playing is equally meant in editions of pieces not so annotated, in Chopin's works as well as in all other music. The ornamenting notes (here written small) should be played pianissimo and with the utmost delicacy of touch. The final triplets should be played with slightly more tone, in the same way as the final notes of a turn ending a trill, while the embellishment notes should be lightly played with the quality of the shake.

Example 97 *a. First measure of theme, and variants. Edited notation.*

The opening half-measure of the theme at *a* occurs again unchanged in form in the 71st measure. In the 3d and 11th measures, *b*, the melodic *A* is embellished with a delicate turn and *B* and *the*, of the original theme are transformed into a triplet by the prefix of the appoggiatura *C*. In the 9th measure at *c*, instead of making a closing triplet, the *C* becomes an acciaccatura-grace-note ornamenting Bb. The variant at *d*, in the 73d measure, is like that at *b* with the turn omitted. Each of these measures should be played so as to make evident to the hearer its derivation from measure 1 at *a*.

The next example contains the measures which follow immediately upon these various entries of the theme. The six eighth-notes of the first measure are succeeded immediately by the notes of the second measure as given below at *a*. Example 98

Second measure of theme and variants. Edited notation.

Here the four times repeated *F* should be unbrokenly sustained by the pedal and fingers for four beats (as indicated by the wholenote within parentheses). In the examples at *b* and *d* this prolonged *F* is struck twice, and at c but once; yet in all four examples the *F*, whether struck once or oftener, sings to the next melodic tone, indicated by a large note, which at a, c, and *d* is *G,* and at *b* is *F.* In the fourth measure at *b* the *F* is embellished by *G* and *Eli,* written in small notes. The second melodic *F* should be sustained by the pedal through the embellishing passage thrown round it until the final triplet, *F, E, E,* is played, with rather more melodic stress.

The notation of the last half of the third and all of the fourth measure, given in this and the preceding *Example,* should be compared with the Mikuli edition of these same measures, shown in *Example 95 a,* where the notes are of equal size, regardless of their greater or less thematic value. Both notations have the same significance and should be rendered in the same way. The slurs connecting the notes are used to group them with regard to a mental subdivision, calculated, with reference to the accompanying harmony, to throw the melody into prominence; and to show the close inner relationship of these passages, which present such unlike appearance to the eye in the original edition, in which they are written in large notes. (The stem connection is here the same as in the original.)

Of this kind of tonal decoration Liszt says: "It is to Chopin we owe... the little groups of superadded notes, falling like drops of pearly dew upon the melodic figure. This species of adornment had hitherto been modeled only upon the *fioriture* of the great Old School of Italian Song; the embellishments for the voice had been servilely copied by the piano, although become stereotyped and monotonous; he imparted to them the charm of novelty, surprise, and variety, unsuited for the vocalist, but in perfect keeping with the character of the instrument." Keats's lines in his *Hyperion* are exquisitely descriptive of such embellishing passages.

"A living death was in each gust of sounds,
Each family of rapturous hurried notes
That fell, one after one, yet all at once,
Like pearl-beads dropping sudden from their string."

The theme is slightly emphasized and given a different color at each entry by the modifications in its outline, by the additions, curtailments, and changes of the chromatic ornamentation which hazily envelops the melody and forms a shimmering setting. At c the first note, *F*, is played with sufficient force for the tone to continue sounding for four beats, until the *G* is heard, introducing the final melodic triplet, *Gb, F, C* (derived from the notes of the original theme at *a* under which they are placed). All notes of the measure should be played evenly; the ornamenting shower of notes should be played pianissimo, and the final triplet may be given with a little more tone.

In the example at *d* the melodic *F* in the second measure is twice struck, and sounds strongly through the dainty embellishing passage of tones, until the final notes of the measure, (?b, *F, E, D*, are played. Of these four notes, the (?b has its own embellishing notes, and the final *F, Eb,* and *D* constitute an interesting triplet on the last beat. The triplet ending seven of the eight measures just analyzed is very characteristic of Chopin, and is to be found in much of his music.

In passage playing it is always well mentally to subdivide the notes into groups, for the sake of a better articulation and also in order to play them more expressively and to bring out the melodic and harmonic outlines. The above grouping of the notes as shown by the slurs is one way of doing this. Another editor might do it quite differently. Klindworth, for instance, instead of using slurs, indicates his grouping by means of additional connecting-tails, making the eighth-notes in measure 74 into sixteenths, as in the following example.

Another might write and play in still another way; but every musician, in his editing and in his rendering, has the bringing out of the original theme in mind, whatever be the means which he may employ to attain this.

Says Rubinstein: "The Pianoforte-Bard, the Pianoforte*Rhapsodist*, the Pianoforte-*Mind*, the Pianoforte-SowZ is Chopin. Expressive Whether the spirit of this instrument breathed tones of

the upon him or he upon it,—how he wrote for it, I harmony do noj. Jmow; Dut onJy an entire going-over-of one-into-the-other could call such compositions into life.... Nor should we overlook the highly interesting fact that he is the only one of the composers who, conscious of his specialty, creates for this specialty (the Pianoforte) and (with the exception of a few songs) attempts no other style of composition.... From a purely musical standpoint, how perfect in technic and form, how interesting and new in harmony, and often how great!"

Although the compositions of Chopin, "the Raphael of the piano," are so strictly pianistic that but few attempts have been made to transcribe them for other instruments, and although in playing his works one should have in mind the pianotone and not the orchestra as in Beethoven-playing, yet there should be much diversity of tone-coloring, and each part or voice should be given with tonal quality, quantity, and duration proportionate to its expressiveness in the passage in which it is found.

"In making an analysis of the work of Chopin," writes Liszt, "we meet with beauties of a high order, expressions entirely new, and a harmonic tissue as original as erudite.... They disguise their profundity under so much grace, their science under so many charms, that it is with difficulty we free ourselves sufficiently from their magical enthralment to judge coldly of their theoretical value.... A high rank must be assigned by the future historians of music to the one who distinguished himself in art by a genius for melody so rare, by such songful and remarkable' enlargements of the harmonic tissue."

Huneker writes that the pianist Halle "was bewildered when he first heard Chopin play, for he did not believe such music could be represented by musical signs."

Schumann in one of his criticisms makes this pregnant statement: "The older I grow, the more convinced I am that the pianoforte is especially prominent in three leading qualities peculiar to it — fulness and variety in exemplification of harmony (made use of by

Beethoven and Franz Schubert), pedal effect (as with Field), and volubility (Czerny, Herz, etc.). The large, broad player exhibits the first, the fantastic artist gives the second, a pearly touch displays the third quality. Manysided, cultured composer-performers, like Hummel, Moscheles, and, finally, Chopin, combine all these, and are consequently the most admired by players; those writers and performers who neglect to study any of these fall into the background. Lowe, indeed, makes use of all; but he is not a fine player, and mind will not do everything."

Mind will not do everything; it is not sufficient that the performer understands and mentally hears the composition he is rendering, that he "should be able to solfa it without the piano," and that his imagination "should be cultivated to the point of retaining the harmony that is given to a melody quite as well as the melody itself"; but it is also necessary that he shall have the skill to communicate his conception of the piece to the listener and to interpret it audibly. In order to make the harmonic scheme evident to the hearer, the accompaniment in this Nocturne, strictly pianistic in form, should be considered as representing a number of voices of various coloring. In the beginning of the piece there are five voices played by the left hand. Each of these voices is found, in the main, in the same place in each group: that is, the first note of each group of six notes is the bass-note, the next voice is found in the second note of each group, etc., though this is not invariably so, for sometimes the voices should be conceived as crossing each other, as they might do in a string quartet. Occasionally, too (as in measures 60—67), the bass-note is not the lowest written note of the group, but is an unwritten prolongation from the preceding measure; while again (as in measures 68-71) the lowest and last note of each group, not the first, is the bass-note of the five following notes.

The first nine measures of the accompaniment are represented in solid chords in the next example, so that a correct conception of the full harmony of each arpeggiated chord may be facilitated; also that it may easily be perceived that while certain voices move interestingly others hold long-sustained tones. In this form, too, the most characteristic notes of the harmony can more readily be discovered.

These measures contain the harmonic skeleton of the arpeggiated chords in the lower staff, shown in *Examples* 102-105, and reveal to the eye that the first Characteristic four measures are founded on a double pedal-tones of the point in the bass on the tonic and dominant notes narmony of the key in which the piece is written — Bb *minor;* and that the bass in the next three measures alternates between *D* and *G,* tonic and subdominant notes of the relative key of *Db major,* into which there is a short modulation; also that for four measures and a half the highest voice sustains *F,* and before this has ceased sounding the next highest voice attacks a prolonged *D.* In the above example the dark notes, and in *Examples* 102-105 the large black-headed notes with double stems, are those most expressive in each harmony, and if played with sufficient prominence they bring out the character of triad, chord of the seventh, chord of the ninth, etc., and also make the best support to the melody, supplementing it and the bass, as shown in *Examples* 83-87.

If these expressive tones be played alone, as shown in *Example* 101, their melodic interest is at once evident. Each of these voices is melodically pleasing in itself, interesting and the minor seconds, duly emphasized in the submelodies playing, are in each case most expressive. These melodic inner voices and the solid chords in which they are found *(Example* 100) should now be compared with the same harmonies in their original arpeggiated form in *Examples* 102-105 and with the same first nine measures of the piece as shown in *Examples* 95 *a* and *b.*

Here again in *Example* 102 are shown in larger notes, connected by curved lines, these same more expressive accompanying notes as they occur in the first three harmonies. In the first arpeg-

giated chord played by the left hand the tones of greatest interest are the melodic *F,* the fundamental *B* and the characteristic minor third of the chord, the *D* in the tenor. The other *F's* and the *B* in the inner voices are merely repetitions in octave of the same tones and are used to fill in the harmony and give it an undulating movement, and should therefore be played pianissimo so as not to interfere with the freshness and beauty of the main tones. The melody, always by far the most expressive voice of a composition, should be brought out with the greatest fulness of tone. Another most important and expressive voice is the bass, which supports not only the melody but the whole composition built upon it. Besides these two voices there usually are the inner voices of considerable interest. In the first arpeggiated chord in *Example* 102, therefore, the tone £b should be made to sing throughout the whole chord, yet without making too much of it. The only way to do this on the pianoforte, where the tone begins to fade away the moment it is produced, is to sound the tone with a little more emphasis than the other less expressive tones of the chord, so that even when not actually connected to the next tone in the same voice it will sound connected, and so form a sub-melody a third (tenth) below the main melody.

In the second half of this measure an arpeggiated chord of the dominant seventh is built upon the pedal-point *RF.* The dissonant seventh, *Eb,* and the leading tone, *A%* are the most characteristic inner tones; but the right hand has a much more important melodic *E* on the sixth beat; therefore, in order not to take away from the interest and novelty of this tone by anticipating it in the left hand (also in order to avoid making a progression of parallel octaves between the melodic *E* in the second measure and *of,* in the third measure and the third note of each of the accompanying arpeggios), the accompanying *El,* should not be sustained over its written value. But the *All,* the leading tone of the key, which sounds so well with the melodic *F,* a sixth above it, and with the other melodic tones which follow,

should be slightly emphasized in order that it may be sustained longer than the duration indicated by the eighth-note stem given it by Chopin. This *A$* likewise makes the expressive progression of a minor second to *B,* the tonic, to which it regularly resolves and which is the most expressive of the inner tones of measure three. The half-note in the melody, the *D,* is best supported, not by a repetition of itself an octave below, but by *By* a tenth below, which, supplemented with the sustained pedal-point in the bass, is the most expressive tone in this harmony. The pedal-point should be held as long as possible by means of the fingers, and afterwards by means of the damper pedal, so as to sustain only the desired chordtones without a perceptible blurring of the melody tones.

Example 103

Measures 3, 4, *and* 5, *edited.*

In the second half of measure 3 all the tones of the chord should be more or less sustained while the original melody, enter ing after a breath, starts again, somewhat more impressively, and repeats in an embellished form the thematic phrase given Embellished hi *Examples* 96 *a* and 102, which at first was an*h«me* nounced simply and without ornamentation. In *Example* 103 the interest of the repeated phrase is heightened by the mystery with which it is surrounded — by the nebulous tone in which it is enveloped—

"Such a soft witchery of sound
As twilight elfins make when they at eve
Voyage on gentle gales to Fairyland."

The embellishing turn thrown round *All* in measure 3 should be lightly played so as to ornament the sustained melodic tone *All.* In the fourth measure the harmonic proportion is similar to that in the second measure. The melodic *F* should be played with considerable emphasis, and the next *F,* preceded by the double appoggiatura *G* and *E,* should be sounded with sufficient strength, so as to be heard singing clearly through the embellishing run woven round it. The pedal should be used to sustain this melodic tone while the run is so lightly played that it is not unpleasantly blurred. "Chopin's fantastic finger plays hither and thither, veiling, unveiling, so that ear and heart long retain the tones." v The notes of the melody should be a little syncopated, as indicated by the vertical dotted-lines connecting the notes of both staves. Yet the notes of the left hand should not be in the least out of time. Moscheles, who in general was out of sympathy with Chopin, writes: "Chopin has just been playing to me, and now for the first time I understand his music. The rubato, which, with his other interpreters, degenerates into disregard of time, is with him only a charming originality of manner; the harsh modulations which strike me disagreeably when I am playing his compositions no longer shock me, because he glides over them in a fairylike way with his delicate fingers. His piano is so soft that he does not need any strong forte to produce his contrasts; and for this reason one does not miss the orchestral effects which the German school requires from a pianoforte player, but allows oneself to be carried away as by a singer who, little concerned about the accompaniment, entirely follows his emotion." Example 104

Measures 5, 6, *and* 7, *edited.*

(meas.6) — (6) (7;

In the sixth measure the five-note inner-melody played by the right hand should be given considerable prominence, and the progression of the two melodies to *F* in the next measure should be felt, while the individuality and songfulness of each should be preserved. To prevent a blurring of these melodies, their tones must be held by means of the fingers, while the pedal should be used with sufficient frequency to sustain accompanying tones.

In order to avoid jeopardizing the interest of the prolonged melodic *F,* to avoid upsetting the tone balance of the harmony by a preponderance of the sharp major third, and Contrapuntal also to avoid the progression of octaves between progression of melody and inner voice, the Gt» of measure 6, V0ices instead of progressing to *F,* should move, with *BF,* to *Al,* in the 7th measure, the accompanying *F's* of this harmony be-

ing most softly played. The pedal should be partially released upon the sounding of the second tone *(BF)* of the second-soprano melody, and be pressed again after the sounding of each melodic tone, so as to sustain the tones of the harmony and connect them with those of the next harmony.

In the first half of measure 7 the most characteristic tone of the inner voices is *Ah,* the fifth of the chord, since root and third are found in bass and melody; as it is also the tone to which the principal tones of the preceding harmony progress, there is every reason that the *A* should be brought into prominence as a tone supporting the melody.

Example 105

Measures 7, 8, *and* 9.

(meas.7) (8) (8)

The measures in the above example contains two somewhat similar motives. In the arpeggiated chord accompanying the first motive in this example the most characteristic inner tones in measure 7 are Gb and *By* F. The (?b progresses in the next measure to *F,* the major third of the harmony, which forms consonant thirds with the bass note *D),* and with the melodic tone *Ah,* and therefore should be played with some importance. Were the character of the harmony alone to be considered, the Bbb would progress distinctly to *A* b in the next measure, but, as the harmonic tendency of the accompanying tones alone is not so important as is their relation to the melody and a proper subordination to it, such a way of playing would here be most undesirable, since it would not only take away from the interest of the melodic *AF,* but would also make an audible succession of parallel octaves between *BW* and *AF* in the melody and an inner voice. Therefore the tone of the accompanying Bbb should cease the moment the melodic Z?bb is sounded, and the accompanying Ab should concede its harmonic rights to *A* b in the melody, an octave above.

The next motive, marked *smorzando* by the composer, modulates in the 9th measure by means of the dominant seventh to *B* minor and introduces a return of the original theme. Although suitably

subordinated to the melody, all the tones of the accompanying harmony in the last half of measure 8 should be played with considerable emphasis, as they are all harmonically interesting. The *E* remains stationary and becomes the seventh of the dominant chord. Through enharmonic change the Bbb becomes *A,* leading-tone of the new key; this tone is, harmonically, the most important of all, because, although it retains the same pitch in both measures, it is so metamorphosed in character as to have an altogether different and new harmonic force. The bass tone (?b progresses to *F* in measure 9. The upper-bass tone Db, in measure 8, should move strongly to *C* in the same measure, and this *C* should be so emphasized and sustained as to avoid the effect of fifths on the accented part of the measure (between bass and upper-bass, (?b and Db to *F* and C), which would occur should the Db move to the *C* in measure 9; the second *C* should be played most softly on this account.

The theme again commences in the second half of measure 9, the harmonic accompaniment being here actually expressed, instead of being understood as at the beginning of the piece.

The composition is in general quiet, dreamy, and rather melancholy, yet does not lack the fire of passion. The first six notes *(Example 102)* should be played in such a Chopin's way as to attract attention to what is to come, tempo rubato They should be played rubato, and with some emphasis, but each melodic tone has its own peculiar coloring, different from that of any of the others, and the beginning of the next measure is rather more subdued and dreamy. The first *F* in each of the measures 2, 4, 12, 72, and 74 should be struck with some force, so as to sound until the closing triplet is played.

In playing the minor seconds, C-D, A-B, G-F, the *C, A* and (?b should be slightly emphasized, as they lean upon the notes following almost with the character of appoggiaturas, rhythmically displaced, as is also the case in the succeeding five variations of the theme, where the harmony is written down, not merely imagined as in the beginning of the piece.

The light runs, iridescent in effect, should be played softly and evenly, although not all of the notes have exactly the same quality, the more expressive being slightly more audible than the others. The melodic *F* should be held by means of the pedal, and the ornamenting runs should be played so lightly that the blurring of tone, scarcely perceptible, adds charm, and the final note of each triplet should have absolutely different coloring from that of the preceding tone, so as to give almost the effect of an appoggiatura to the *D* in the succeeding measure. Although the notes of the embellishing runs should be perfectly even, there should at the same time be a syncopated character to them. An attempt has been made to indicate this by the dotted-lines, which show that the notes of the two hands are not played simultaneously, yet that they should preserve the articulation and grouping indicated by the slurs. These are suggestions as to a way of playing these measures, yet the playing cannot be adequately described in words, and besides, there are many other modes of playing which equally interpret them. There should be no rubato in the left hand,—the freedom must be confined to the melody,—otherwise the result is disorder, not music. Regarding rubato, Mozart wrote to his father in 1777: "My keeping so accurately in time causes them all much surprise. The left hand being quite independent in the *tempo rubato* of our adagio, they cannot at all comprehend. With them the left hand always yields to the right."

Schumann poetically describes the effect of some of Chopin's music in these words: "Imagine that an iEolian harp possessed all the scales, and that an artist's hand struck these with all kinds of fantastic, elegant embellishments, even rendering audible a deep fundamental tone and a softly flowing upper voice — and you will have some idea of his playing. But it would be a mistake to suppose that he allowed us to hear every small note in it; it was rather the undulation of the *A* major chord, brought

out more loudly here and there with the pedal, but exquisitely entangled in the harmony: we followed a wondrous melody in the sustained tones, while in the middle voices a tenor voice broke clearly from the chords, and joined in the principal melody." Liszt, also, speaks of "that floating and indeterminate contour which so fascinates us in his graceful con ceptions"; but he also calls attention to the fact that "richness, often exuberance, never interferes with clearness; the sculpturing is never disordered; the luxury of ornament never overloads the chaste tenderness of the principal lines."

Much has been written about the Chopin *rubato*. His own words have been preserved by his pupils. "The left hand should be like a Capellmeister," said he; "it dare not for a moment become uncertain and wavering." And again: "Let your left hand be your conductor and always keep time." His pupil Mikuli explains the *tempo rubato* in this way: "While the singing hand, either irresolutely lingering or as in passionate speech, eagerly anticipating with a certain impatient vehemence, freed the truth of the musical expression from all rhythmical fetters, the other, the accompanying hand, continued to play strictly in time." Frederick Niecks, in his Life of Chopin, quotes Mme. Streicher, a Chopin pupil, as follows: "His playing was always noble and beautiful, his tones always sang, whether in full forte or in the softest piano. He took infinite pains to teach the pupil this cantabile way of playing. '*Il* (or *elle*) *ne sait pas Her deux notes*' was his severest censure. He also required adherence to the strictest rhythm, hated all lingering and dragging, misplaced rubatos, as well as exaggerated ritardandos. '*Je vois prie de vous asseoir,* ' he said on such an occasion with gentle mockery. And it is just in this respect that people make such terrible mistakes in the execution of his works.... In the use of the pedal he had likewise attained the greatest mastery, was uncommonly strict regarding the misuse of it, and said repeatedly to the pupil, 'The correct employment of the pedal remains a study for life.'"

Next in importance to Chopin's own words are perhaps those of Liszt, whose interpretations of Chopin's works were sometimes more satisfactory to the composer than his own. Liszt gave this explanation to a pupil: "Do you see those trees? The wind plays in the leaves, stirs up life among them, but the *tree remains the same.* That is the Chopin *rubato.*"... "Through his peculiar style of performance, Chopin imparted the constant rocking with the most fascinating effect, thus making the melody undulate to and fro, like a skiff driven on over the bosom of tossing waves. This manner of execution, which set a seal so peculiar upon his own style of playing, was at first indicated by the term *tempo rubato,* affixed to his writings, a *tempo* agitated, broken, interrupted, a movement flexible, yet at the same time abrupt and languishing and vacillating as the flame under the fluctuating breath by which it is agitated. In his later productions we no longer find this mark. He was convinced that if the performer understood them he would divine this rule of irregularity. All his compositions should be played with this accentuated and measured swaying and balancing. It is difficult for those who have not frequently heard him play to catch this secret of their proper execution. He seemed desirous of imparting this style to his numerous pupils, particularly those of his own country."

The most broadly practical as well as the most musicianly and the most scholarly discussion of this subject which has yet Paderewski on appeared in print is to be found in Finck's *Success* tempo rubato *in Music and How it is Won,* in the eight pages which Paderewski has written for this volume on *Tempo Rubato.* This article clarifies all which has been written by others, and is the greatest utterance upon the subject.

CHAPTER XI

Orchestration At The Pianoforte

Raff says that "the elements of Orchestration are those of painting. The composition per *se* represents the design; the melody, the outline; harmony, the light and Elements of shade; and instrumentation, the coloring." These orchestration elements should be as evident in pianoforte playing as in the rendering of orchestral music. To orchestrate pieces at the pianoforte needs musicianship; for no matter how fully phrased and expressively marked a piece may be, there is always much left to the performer's knowledge and taste, because adequate orchestration is impossible of notation in pianoforte music.

In beginning the study of a composition, its general character, the key in which it is written, the measure signature and the figuration should be noted. Then its formal structure should be analyzed, for, to quote Schumann, "Only when the form is entirely clear to you will the spirit become clear." Not only should the general design be observed (it may be that of Rondo, Sonata, Fugue, or other musical form, with characteristic divisions, themes, modulations, transitions, episodes, strettos, codas, etc.), but also the minutest details of thematic development, the inversions, repetitions, contractions, augmentations, curtailments, and elaborations of a theme; as well as the rhythms, phrasings, signs and terms of expression used.

Of equal importance is the treatment of the melody, for there is no music without melody. The player must be able to detect the notes of this voice, even if they are intertwined with those of many other voices. As has been seen, the melody may range from very high to very low tones, the notes running thread-like through the other voices, unrecognized by the pianist, if his perception be not quickened by theoretical knowledge. This intermixture of notes of the different voices may make it difficult, even impossible, for the editor to indicate by marks (such as additional stems, rests, notes of large size, slurs, accents, etc.) the location of these notes of the melody, upon the correct rendering of which the beauty of the composition so largely depends. The melodic notes may be of smaller size than others, in the form of acciaccatura-gracenotes; or they may be written as sixty-fourth-notes or as eighth-notes, and yet

be intended by the composer to be long sustained. But, when the melody is found, it should be rendered, if cantabile in character, with such touch as will make the tones richly vocal, in imitation of human song; if the melody be instrumental in character, it should be given in imitation of the tone of a violin, horn, or other instrument, or of a combination of instruments.

Not less essential is it that the expressive tones of the harmony should be brought out with more prominence than the less characteristic tones,—the basstones with their own peculiar lights and shades, and other essential tones which, when given prominence, draw out the beauties of the harmonies. One should hear the contrapuntal progression of the different voices, and, more distinctly than less expressive tones, the dissonances, followed, more softly, by their resolutions. Often it is the third of the triad, sometimes poetically called its soul, which is the characteristic tone. But the selection for tonal prominence of expressive and therefore important tones of the harmony depends not only upon the nature of the chords themselves and their mutual relation, butalso upon what melodic tones are played with them and what characteristic effects are intended by the composer to be produced.

Music played on the pianoforte depends largely for its poetry and beauty of interpretation upon the employment of an expressive variety of tone-color. By instrumentation at the pianoforte is meant, not that the auditor is conscious of an imitation of the violoncello, the horn, or the oboe (although this is sometimes the case), but that he is aware of different qualities of tone. These are attained by the performer through his vivid preconception of an ideal coloring of each tone. If the composition is instrumental in character, the mental picture which he strives to reproduce upon the pianoforte is usually an orchestral one, and a finer tonal variety is attained than if the player thinks merely of the pianotone. Says Berlioz, in *Modern Instrumentation and Orchestration:* "Considered as a small orchestra in it-

self, the pianoforte should have its own appropriate instrumentation. It evidently has one; and this art forms a portion of the pianist's. It is his duty, on many occasions, to judge if it be requisite to render certain parts prominent, while others are left in shadow; and if he ought to play conspicuously an intermediate passage, by giving lightness to the upper ornamentals, and less force to the bass." As a simple illustration of instrumentation at the pianoforte, let us transcribe for orchestra this pianistic figure:

Example 106 considering it as the first of a long series of measures in which there is a double organ-point on the same or on different notes, and a continuous, undulating movement, such as would be suitable accompaniment to a barcarolle or a slumber-song. What instruments would sound well? As one of many possible arrangements, imagine the first two notes, which constitute a double pedal-point in the bass, played by violoncelli, while another instrument notes melodically, thus: a horn, perhaps — takes the same Now a violoncello solo, plays these notes in the tenor: which is another notation of the original figure, and a more elaborate representation of the effect desired, which is to be brought about in playing on the pianoforte by a judicious use of the pedals and of the fingers.

It is apparent that the instrumentation of but six notes of accompaniment gives considerable variety of tone-color, and that even so slight and apparently uninteresting a group of notes as that in *Example* 106 may represent not one voice only but many voices. All of these voices should be played with due recognition of their relative values and in imitation of their conceived orchestral character; and all should be subordinated to the melody when it enters. Orchestral changes of tone-coloring should frequently be imagined and imitated in pianoforte playing, for even if the rendition does not convey to the auditor the effects striven for by the performer, it does give each voice suggestive and individual interest and make of the whole composition a well-balanced and characteristic unit. The instrumentation should be varied, or the playing will become monotonous. In particular, one should make sparing use of the soft pedal and of unusual pedal effects of any kind, or they become tiresome.

Instrumentation is absolutely essential to the correct rendering of piano compositions by Bach, Beethoven and Liszt. Source of the Although variety of tone-color is equally needed in poetic the playing of Chopin's music, his compositions inspiration are go innately pianistic that one does not think of the orchestra in playing them, any more than he did in writing them. Coloring, in Chopin's works, is to be considered more as in imitation of orchestral variety of tone than as color orchestrally conceived; this is, in a measure, true also of Schumann's works.

The above few principles of pianistic orchestration are illustrated in two of Mendelssohn's *Songs without Words,* each of which is founded, in the main, upon an organ-point. The *Venetian Gondola-Songs* in *F# minor* and in *G minor,* souvenir of Mendelssohn's visit to Venice, are fine examples of the regular form, good harmonies and agreeable melodies of his *Songs without Words.* Properly to interpret any romantic composition, the performer must have a vivid idea of it, and the imagination is here assisted by the title, which, though it does not aim to convey specific images, yet suggests the poetry of melody and of motion upon the water. The player cannot but think he sees the waters of the Grand Canal, reflecting in the soft moonlight the marble of the Venetian palaces, and the many moving boats, whose somber coloring serves as a foil to the gaily dressed and picturesque gondoliers. The sound of music is heard, now close by, now from a distance; sometimes it is the song of the gondoliers, again it comes from the occupants of the boats, who accompany their voices with guitar or mandolin. In some such surroundings these beautiful little compositions may have been written, although, as Beethoven remarks in a preface to his *Pastoral Symphony,* they are "more expression of feeling than painting."

V As interpretation of a piece of music depends both upon correct conception of it and upon a mechanical skill sufficient to convey this conception to others, considerable **w** . Conception attention should be devoted to a minute analysis of its rhythmic structure, its melody and its harmonies, as well as to the acquisition of a technic which will enable the performer to make these elements of orchestration at the pianoforte felt and enjoyed by the hearer. By means of notes of contrasting size and blackness; of additional stems, slurs and dynamic signs, the orchestration — that is, the effect desired by the composer— is suggested more completely in *Examples* 112-117 at *b* than in the original edition at *a,* which is written, as is customary, in the simplest pianistic notation, and consequently with much left to the intuition of the performer.

The song in *F§ minor,* of which the first seven measures are given in *Example* 108, is founded upon the keynote, the F# Tonic in the bass; and the harmonies in the third and pedai-point the fourth measure should not be considered as dominant harmony with C# for the bass-note, but as dominant harmony built upon the organ-point *F§.* Example 107

Chopin — Berceuse.

In this respect it is somewhat similar in form to Chopin's *Berceuse,* where in each of its seventy measures the first Db is the bass-note for both tonic and dominant chords. If they were conceived and played as two different chords with different bass-notes, this poetic and dreamy accompaniment would sound very thin and commonplace. The bass note *D,* marked with a staccato dot, sounds softly and continuously throughout the entire composition.

Example 108

Mendelssohn — Gondola-Song, in F# minor.

In the Mendelssohn Barcarolle the notes played by the left hand naturally divide themselves into several voices of different color values. The lowest F# and C# constitute a double pedal-point, which, with the undulating and even flow of the rest of the musical figure in the left

hand, sug-Double gests the rocking and the placid drifting of the pedal-point boat. The notes of the higher voices move but slightly at first, then in the fifth and sixth measures progress more actively. Each voice should have an individual characteristic coloring.

The tones of most of the voices have a longer duration than their notation might seem to indicate. The double organpoint F# and C# and the rest of the accompaniment in the left hand are more fully notated in *Example 109,* so as to call, attention to the many voices and their varied coloring.

Example 109

Edited notation of measures 1, 2 *and* 3.

(meSn (2) (8

The tones of the moving voices in *Example 108* should be connected. Even if the hand be so small that the fingers cannot remain upon the keys long enough to sustain one tone until another is produced, yet the tones can be made to sound legato. As much as possible the finger should be relied upon for obtaining legato, supplementing with the damper pedal, which should be pressed lightly so as to keep the tone pure, for when the pedal is pressed entirely down, so as to free the strings completely from the restraint of the dampers, the sympathetic vibration of all the strings produces many harmonics, some of which, distantly related to the tone played, intrude upon it, making the sound too thick and lacking in purity. In cantabile playing especially, the pedal should be released and depressed at the right moment, so as not to blur a single tone. It may be well at first to study the accompaniment alone, playing it with both hands, as suggested in *Examples* 3 and 100, for this will give the player clearer conception of the harmonies and their progressions; afterwards the qualities of touch employed by the two hands should be imitated by the left hand alone. It is desirable to play the accompaniment in the form both of chords and of arpeggiated harmonies, so as to enjoy their full flavor and richness, the essential tones of each harmony, and their relative dynamic values, as well as to produce a good balance of all the voices.

In order to mark the reentrance of the first theme in measure 36, there should be a slight detachment of the notes Reentry of *A* and *B* from those preceding, as indicated by theme the breath-mark placed between the phrases.

The notes beginning the theme anew should be played with a firmer touch than those closing the preceding phrase, in imitation of a singer who takes a breath and begins another and an interesting phrase to which the attention of the auditor is directed. The crescendo of the trill should not be made too rapidly nor should too much tone be used, and the final tones of the trill should not be hurried.

In measure 39 *(Example* 110) the hand should no longer be inclined in scale position, as it is here the little finger which Position of should have a favorable position upon the keys; *bani* the wrist may be turned a little inward, weight ing the hand slightly on the outside, as though to strike the sustained C# with the fifth finger before the thumb strikes its C# an octave below; this, indeed, may actually be done at first, in practicing, until the position becomes an easy one; the moving voice, as part of the theme, should be quite prominent.

Example 111 *9 §*

In the coda *(Example* 111) the descending melody, F#, *E, D,* C#, *B, B,* C#, *A,* and its repetition in the succeeding measures, should be heard distinctly and be fuller in tone than the bass tones, while these last should be more prominent than their octaves played with the thumb.

At the close of the piece (112 a) Mendelssohn intends the full harmony in the third measure from the end to continue sounding through the succeeding measures, for it would be a very poor orchestration of this composition to end it with two Fiji's three octaves apart and no intervening

Correct concep-..,.,,, tionofthe harmony; it might remind one of the passage meaning of the m the Berlioz *Requiem* which represents the yawning of hell by means of three flutes and eight unison trombones and nothing else. *Ex-*

ample 112 *b* shows how the notes at *a* should sound. As in *Examples* 2, 3, 113, 116 and 117, the rests at *a* are placed by the composer as guides for the fingers, not for the tone.

Example 113

Mendelssohn — Gondola-song, in G minor.

a. Original notation.

The *Gondola-song, in G minor,* may be orchestrated in a manner somewhat similar to that of the one in F# *minor.* The pedal-point and the rest of the accompaniment in the left hand should be mentally instrumented by the student so as to obtain orchestral coloring when it is played. The *G* and *D* constitute at the same time stationary tones and part of a melodic figure, as did the F# and C# in the other song. Although of less prominence than the bass *G* and the chords 0rchestration on the second and fifth beats of the measures, the elaborately D played by the left hand should have throughout notated the piece its own subdued importance, so that in combination with the bass tone *G* it may give a vivid impression of the rocking of the gondola upon the waves. The accompaniment, as shown by the rests in measure 1, *Example* 113, as first played by both hands, is the same as that written in the seventh and succeeding measures for the left hand alone.

The dots over the *G* in measure 7 do not in this instance call for staccato but for slight emphasis; they also help to call attention to the fact that the notes over which Meaning of they are placed constitute a voice separate from *fbe* dot the voices represented by the other notes; and they denote a rest for the finger, not for the tone. The tones of the accompaniment are soft in comparison with those of the melody, yet the progression of the inner voices of the harmony should be heard, the upper voice forming a sub-melody in the tenor, as shown by the large notes in *Examples* 113 *b,* 115 *b* and 117 *b.*

The expressiveness and consequent value of the sustained *D's* should be fully realized. The effect is so beautiful when the *D* of the melody is prolonged from the fifth ,,

" r t Expressiveness measure into the seventh, that it should be played of sustained as shown at *b,* even though rests be marked. This tone *D* may be imagined as the stroke of a bell coming over the water to the occupants of the gondola, the prolonged vibrations fading gradually away into silence.

Example 114 a continues the composition begun in *Example* 113 a, and gives an edited notation — a fuller orchestration — of the notes played by the right hand at *b.* The *D* in the 11th measure continues sounding until it moves to *C* on the third beat of the 13th measure. With a skilled touch the effect of a sustained *D* connecting smoothly with *C* can be obtained, notwithstanding the renewed attack of the *D* at the beginning of measure 13. To attain this effect the *D* may be sounded with sonority in measure 11, and held with the pedal while playing very softly the *D* written as a quarter-note in measure 13. If desired, the same effect may be produced in some degree in measure 9, for the melodic *D* struck in measure 5, *Example* 113, should still continue to sound faintly in measures 7 and 8.

In measures 32 and 33 the imitations in the tenor and alto should be well brought out. The *D* on the fourth beat of the thirty-third measure belongs to both tenor and alto, as shown at *b,* and should be held in the alto voice until the *C* is played on the sixth beat, while, in order not to interfere with this progression of the voice, the lowest *D* on the sixth beat of measure 33 should be played pianissimo, as in measures 9 and 13, *Example* 114 *a.* Example 116

a. Original edition.

In *Example* 116 the right hand should play the *D's* in octaves very softly, while, to prevent the harmony from sounding thin and empty, great prominence should be □, silent presgiven to *D* and *G,* which should be sustained as sure of a key indicated by the dotted-half-notes inserted in the edition of the passage given at *b.* After playing the last octaves in the right hand in measure 39, the sustained *D* and *G* should be prolonged by the finger instead of by the pedal, which, when raised at the beginning of measure 40, will release the *G.* as demanded by the above notation, while the finger sustains the tone *D.* The sign I I indicates the silent pressure of a finger upon a key which previously has been struck and released by the finger while the tone produced was sustained by the pedal. The tone can be prolonged independently of the pedal by this silent pressure of a key, and the sign for its use is given in measures 37 and 39. Further explanation of this effect is given with *Examples* 152, 153 and 154. The counter-melody in the tenor should not be ignored, especially in measures 38 and 39, where, if the third of the triad, *BF,* is not well brought out, the harmony sounds bare —too much *a la Palestrina* to be suitable to this style of composition. That Mendelssohn desired sustained tone in these measures is indicated by his words, *sempre pedale,* in measure 36. (See*sempre pedale,* in Chapter XII, The Pedals.)

A composition performed without variety of tone is far from enjoyable. What an unendurable effect if this composition Orchestral were played by wood-wind only! Of all orchestral coloring. instruments it is to the strings alone that we are instrumentation content to listen long without desiring other coloring. How we enjoy string quartets! It follows that in playing on the pianoforte, which is the orchestra of the pianist, if he would not become tedious the performer must have fine color contrast. Where the *D* is prolonged through several measures it may sometimes be imagined as begun by a horn and then continued by the wood-wind, by this means changing the color without, apparently, a fresh attack of tone — an effect very common in orchestral music.

The whole piece is purely instrumental in character, and so each of the final *D's* in measures 44 and 45 should have a special color and should be supported by the superlegato harmony of the preceding measure. The first melodic *D* may be imagined as played by the horn, and the second as an echo by the clarinets. The D's in the next to the last measure may be attacked with the third finger, which may lie rather flatly on the key and be drawn off forward with a downward pressure from gradually raised wrist and forearm. This touch gives fresh color to the tone, which may be modified still further by trilling the pedal lightly, so as to change the quantity and quality of the vibrations and yet to sustain the bass and accompanying tones. The *D* in the last measure might be similarly played, but with less pressure, more softly, and with a very leisurely stroke of the finger upon the key. The soft pedal may be employed, more to obtain its inherent peculiar coloring than to aid in the pianissimo. The final bass-note, *G,* should not have such prominence that it seems to descend melodically from the *D* played by the right hand, for the composer desires, not a perfect close on the tonic, but a close with the fifth as final melodic tone. This beautiful effect is often destroyed by the ignorant or careless player, just as in the singing of the tragic song, *In Questa Tomba,* the effect desired by Beethoven is sometimes entirely lost by the descent of the voice from the closing fifth indicated to the tonic, the singer forgetting that liberties which may be taken with a light trifle are out of place in a great composition.

CHAPTER XII

The Pedals

Rubinstein with doubtful rhetoric but very deep significance calls the pedal the soul of the pianoforte. He says: "I The soul of the consider the art of properly using the pedal as the piano most difficult problem of higher piano playing; and if we have not yet heard the piano at its best, the fault possibly lies in the fact that it has not been fully understood how to exhaust the capabilities of the pedal.... The more I play the more thoroughly I am convinced that the pedal is the soul of the piano; there are cases where the pedal is everything'."

Owing to the ever-increasing sonority of the modern pianoforte, the possibilities inherent in the pedals have been rapidly Development of developed during the last half-century and espethe piano cially in the last generation, for it is due to the augmented tone-power of the piano that the pedal mechanism for controlling the quantity, quality and duration of sound is continually being improved by the best piano-makers. Many patents hitherto possessed exclusively by a great piano-house have recently expired, and the number of medium-priced pianos with facilities for artistic performance hitherto found only in those of the most expensive makes is growing steadily. These instruments demand of the performer not only manual dexterity but also a highly developed pedal technic.

Accurate knowledge of the purposes of the pedals and of the means employed by artists to achieve those purposes are Pedal usage necessary to the twentieth-century pianist, for difficult to teach while artistic use of the pedals is a gift, the correct use should be acquired by every pianist; and much that popularly passes as artistic employment of the pedals dependent upon talent consists merely in a correct use which may be acquired by any one who is properly taught. When we take into consideration the enormous mass of exercises and studies written for the education of the fingers in piano playing, it seems a little remarkable that so few works are devoted to the training of the music student in a correct use of the pedal, for the art of properly managing the pedal *is* the most difficult problem of higher piano playing. This fact must in the near future call forth the supply as it has already brought the demand for systematized studies relating to the pianoforte pedals, for teachers are beginning to appreciate the Russian master's declaration: "Of all the elements of a correct performance upon the piano, I consider the proper use of the pedal as the most difficult to acquire and to impart. It pertains strictly to the higher art of piano playing. The best of us have room for improvement in this direction. If, as I believe, we have not yet heard the best of which the piano is capable, it is because the artistic possibilities which lie in the pedal have not as yet been fully understood by either pianists or composers for the piano." Yet, although of all forms of piano technic the control of the pedal is the most difficult to acquire and *to impart,* even now, in so far as the writer has been able to ascertain, there are but few publications which treat of the subject, either as a side issue in a scant few pages, or more fully in special handbooks.

The authorities of the first half of the nineteenth century, Mozart's pupil Hummel and Beethoven's pupil Czerny, each in his *Grand School for the Pianoforte* devotes Bibliography of chapters to the use of the pedal of his day, but *the* Pedals these books are now of but little practical value as guides to the student of piano playing, although historically they are of great interest to the musician, as are also the historical surveys of pedal mechanism and development found in *The History of the Pianoforte* by the late A. J. Hipkins, and his various articles in *Grove's Dictionary of Music* and in the *Encyclopaedia Britannica.*

The first modern musician to write about and give exercises for the pedal was Louis Kohler, who in the first volume of his *Systematische Lehrmethode,* published in 1856, "laid down definite principles for the use of the pedal." This work he followed, in 1861, with *Der Klavier Unterricht,* in which he deKohiers pioneer votes a chapter of eight pages to *Der Pedalge*worksontne *brciuch,* and makes reference to the pedal in scatpedal tered paragraphs. His *Technische Kunstlerstudien,*

Op. 147, Vol. I, contains nineteen pages of studies for the pedal. Of this last Liszt wrote to the author in 1875: "The entrance of the pedal *after* the striking of the chords as indicated by you to the utmost extreme, seems to me an ingenious idea, the application of which is greatly to be recommended to pianoforte players, teachers and composers, especially in slow *tempi.* In 1882 Kohler published *Der Klavier Pedalzug, seine Natur und kunstlerische Anwendung* (The Pedal, its Nature and Artistic Application), a pamphlet of 132 pages embodying and extending the teachings of his previous works. It is greatly to be regretted that this original and valuable work is not obtainable in the English language.

The only comprehensive treatise on the pedals of the modern pianoforte is that of Hans Schmitt, of the Conservatory Hans schmitt's of Vienna. Published in the German language book in 1875, it was translated into English eighteen years later by Frederick S. Law, and published under the title of *The Pedals of the Pianoforte.* This is a masterly scientific treatise which clearly explains the mechanism of the pianoforte action and the theory of vibration in so far as it applies to pianoforte playing. The book contains original examples of various functions of the pedals including the utilization of harmonics, and many short illustrative extracts from classic music. It covers the entire field of theoretical pedal study, and will remain the standard work so long as there are no radical changes in or additions to the pianoforte as we know it. Nothing new has been added to this branch of pedal literature, but several books have appeared, some of which are excellent, though none have added materially to what is to be found in Schmitt's great work, concerning which Liszt wrote: "It is well known how much mischief is done to the piano both with hands and feet.

May your instructive pamphlet on the right use of the pedal duly benefit pianoforte players."

Schmitt refers to a brochure which the author has been unable to obtain— *L'Ame du Piano,* by Alfred Quidant. There are also a dozen admirable pages concerning the Other theoretical pedals in Adolf Kullak's *Esthetics of Pianoforte* treatises *Playing,* and some good suggestions in his *Art of Touch.* Albert F. Venino is the author of *A Pedal Method,* which was published in 1893, and the year 1897 produced *A Guide to the Proper Use of the Pianoforte Pedals, with examples from out of the historical concerts of Anton Rubinstein, translated from the German by John A. Preston,* and *The Pedals,* two books by Hugh A. Kelso. Julius R. Weber published in *The Musician* for December, 1903, a monograph on *Methods and Signs for the Use of the Pianoforte Pedals;* Frederick S. Law in *The Musical Observer* of June and July, 1910,

has eight columns entitled *A Study of the Damper Pedal and Its Significance in Artistic Piano Playing;* Marie Prentner has four pages on Pedaling in her book *The Leschetizky Method,* 1903; Malwine Bree in her book *The Groundwork of the Leschetizky Method,* 1902, has three pages on *The Pedal,* and Marie Unschuld, in *The Pianist's Hand,* 1909, gives four pages to the use of the pedal. On the same subject is a chapter of thirteen pages in *Fundamental Technics,* by Mason and Mathews, Ditson, 1905, and Clayton Johns in his *Essentials of Piano Playing,* Ditson, 1909, devotes five pages to the pedal. Eight pages of vital and practical value in regard to pedal usage are contained in Josef Hofmann's *Piano Playing,* 1908. These publications are all interesting to read, and are of value to the experienced musician, but they are not systematized books of instruction containing ample material for practice.

The only exhaustive work published on the subject is that of Albino Gorno, of the College of Music of Cincinnati. His work, the first edition of which was published in Albino Gomo's 1894 and the last in 1900, is entitled *Material* pedal studies *for the Study of the Pianoforte Pedals,* and may be called the practical counterpart of Schmitt's complete theoretical treatise. It is in three parts. Part I deals exclusively with the damper pedal; Part II introduces the soft pedal used alone and in combination with the damper pedal; Part III (in manuscript) adds to these the use of the sostenuto pedal and, besides original studies of great interest, gives as examples classic and modern compositions entire, which illustrate all possible effects producible by the pedals singly and together, in connection with touches of different kinds. The first studies are simple but musical, and consist in connecting chords by means of the pedal, the use of which is indicated by Kohler's precise notation. By natural gradations the pupil is exercised in all uses of the pedals, even those little known to pianists in general. This is the only published work in which the indicated use of the pedals is obligatory to a correct rendering of the music, the fingers alone being unable to obtain the desired effects. While examining this work in manuscript, in 1888, the eminent pianist Rosenthal smilingly exclaimed: "Why, you have here noted down for the use of pupils many effects which I had thought were secrets of my own." Hans von Billow also expressed profound interest in these studies, especially in those written for the sostenuto pedal.

There are other publications intended for the use of students, all of interest, but none of these add anything to what is found in the seventy-five pages of the Gorno Pedal Studies, and no one else covers the ground nearly so thoroughly; and in no other pedal work is there such genuine flow of spontaneous melody and delightful harmony.

The other works intended for students' practice are Dr. Hugo Riemann's *Studies in Pedal Usage, Op. 39, Book V,* 1895; other pedal Arthur Whiting's *Pianoforte Pedal Studies,* 1904; studies Arthur Foote's *Two Pianoforte Pedal Studies,* 1885; Felix Smith's 36 *Short Pedal Studies,* 1899; Orla Rosenhoff's *Little Studies for the Pedal;* Kunkel's *Piano Pedal Method,* 1893; Jessie Gaynor's *First Pedal Studies,* 1906; W. S. Sprankle's *The Piano Pedal,* 1894; Ludwig Schytt6's *Pedal Studies,* 1894; W. S. B. Mathews's *School of the Piano Pedal,* Ditson, 1906; Carl Faelten's *Pedal Exercises for the Pianoforte,* 1900, and Mrs. A. M. Virgil's *The Piano Pedals,* 1912.

The modern player who is ambitious of commendable art must not be content with a haphazard use of the pedal and with clever imitation. The study of the pedals is Definite knowiexacting and requires accurate knowledge of the edge desirable action of the piano, thorough understanding of the music to be played, a definite conception of the effect to be produced, and why this effect is a desirable or an indispensable one. It is indeed surprising how little the average student of piano playing concerns himself with the mechanism of his instrument, yet some knowledge of the action and function of keys, hammers

and dampers is essential before attempting to employ the pedals.

The cut on page 160 is from a photograph of a workingsection of the action of a grand piano. The supporting black framework below and to the right of the action is not found in the piano, but is used here merely to hold this small section of the action together and to form a place of attachment for the few inches of horizontal wire string shown in the upper right-hand corner of the picture.

In the middle and upper registers of the piano there are three unison strings to each tone. In a lower register there are two unison strings to a tone, and the lowest tones KeySj ham. are produced from one string. Each *key* (K) is a mersdampers lever which, when pressed by the finger, acts upon other levers/and raises simultaneously a *hammer* (H) and a *damper* (D).vThe oval hammer, which lies below either one string or below two or three unison strings, is made of rather hard felt stretched upon a wooden hammer-head. The *damper* (D), which lies upon the *string* (S) or unison strings, consists of cushions of very soft felt depending from a wooden damperhead which is upheld by a vertical wire (DW), as is shown at the right of the figure. When a key is struck its hammer rises and comes into more or less forceful contact with the corresponding string, causing it to vibrate and produce a musical tone, and at the same time the damper is raised from the string, leaving it free to vibrate so long as the finger remains THE ACTION OF A GRAND PIANO

A, action bracket; B, back check; D, damper; g damper lever; DW, damper wire; H, hammer; HS, hammer-stem; J, jack; K, key; L, repetition lever; R, roller; S, string upon the key, although the sound gradually dies away. When the finger is removed from the key before vibration has ceased, the damper falls upon the string, stopping sound instantly.

v The final motion of the hammer attack upon the string is caused by the slipping of the piece of wood known as the *jack* (J), under and back of a cylindrical *roller* (R) of .....-T....., Repetition action buckskin-covered felt. In the illustration

its circular end is to be seen just under the stem of the hammer, and touching it, below, is the *jack,* which is always perpendiculai lo the *hammer-stem* (HS) when, as here, the key is not pressed and the hammer remains at its lowest point. When the key is pressed down, the jack, after causing the hammer to strike the string, escapes back of the roller, and the hammer remains at rest at some point nearer the string than is shown in the figure. This upward movement of the jack against the roller and escapement behind it completes the blow of the hammer in every case, no matter how the key is touched or what quality of tone is produced. If the finger presses the key rather slowly, the weight of the hammer is felt in its resistance to the movement of the jack as it passes under the roller. This slight weight, which is experienced in the touch of all good pianos, is an unerring guide to the trained finger, especially in cantabile playing, and through proper management of it much refinement of tone may be obtained. The *roller* and the *jack* are parts of the mechanism which make it possible to repeat a tone quickly and as many times as desired; for when the key is allowed to rise but slightly, although the jack slips back into its former position, the hammer does not return to its original place, but remains very near the strings; and the *damper* remaining off the strings, there is no discontinuance of tone between repeated strokes of the same key.

It is the function of the *damper pedal* to raise all the dampers (D) from all the strings upon which they lie, and also to lower the dampers upon the strings. The dampers are raised by pressing the foot upon the pedal, and are lowered by removing the pressure. All tones sounding or produced while the pedal is pressed down will continue until pedal pressure is removed, when the soft felt of the dampers falling upon the strings instantly checks vibration and stops the sound. In the figure the forefinger has been used to move that part of the action which in the pianoforte proper is moved by pedal pressure, and consequently the dampers are shown raised from the strings.

The fingers and the pedal are interdependent. Preceding examples have shown that there are many effects which can be Pedal eSects ob-accomplished only when the pedal is applied to tained by fingers connect or to sustain tone. The reverse also is true, that many fine and indispensable effects of sustained tone would be impossible were it not for a clever and silent manipulation of fingers upon keys previously struck so as to cause an uninterrupted continuance of tone which the damper pedal had sustained. Such effects of tone sustained by the fingers instead of by the pedal might well be called pedal effects obtained by the fingers, for this phrase helps to recall the fact that while the pedal is a lever by means of which all the dampers are raised collectively from the strings and are lowered upon them, each key also is a lever which raises and lowers a single one of these dampers in the same manner as the damper pedal raises and lowers them all. In other words, the pedal is a complete damping mechanism operated by the foot, and each key, besides being a tone-producing medium, is a partial damping mechanism operated by the fingers. A downward pressure of the pedal raises all the dampers from all the strings. A downward pressure of any one key, whether or not productive of tone, raises one damper from the one string or from the two or three unison strings upon which it lies.

A key can be pressed down quickly or slowly, with much or with little force, and with various gradations and combinations of speed and force. As long as a key is depressed, even slightly, by the finger, the damper remains somewhat raised above the string and the hammer does not fall back quite to its original position. The more rapidly and the more vigorously a key is depressed, the more *martellato* and attacked the resultant tone, and the further the hammer rebounds from the strings, there being, in good pianos, several different places of rest for the hammer, which are the result of different ways of attacking the key and of keeping the finger in control of the key after depressing it. A hammer is

at its lowest point and greatest distance from the strings when the key is not depressed by the finger. A rather slow and not too vigorous depression of the key, the finger remaining on it, leaves the hammer very near to the strings, which by means of controlled key-pressure may be sounded with sonority and with a minimum of hammer-attack on strings and of finger-attack upon key, sounds which often mar the tone produced. A quicker and more forcible depression of the key drops the hammer to a point of rest between these two just mentioned.

It is frequently stated in print that the quality of a tone once produced cannot be altered by further manipulation of the key which produced it. Nothing could be Variety of tone farther from the truth. Much variety is produced producible after by this very means, as can be both heard and seen striking key in the playing of artists and especially in the interpretations of those wizards of the keyboard who enchant by masterly rendering of a poetic conception.

When key-pressure has produced tone by causing the hammer to strike and the damper to rise from the string or unison strings, this tone, while gradually dying away, may be sustained and much altered in quality and somewhat altered in quantity through judicious and several times repeated use of the pedal in rapid alternation with silent finger-pressure upon the key, since both of these are methods which keep the damper raised. The tone generated while the pedal is pressed down is full, rich and vibrant with overtones, since the pedal keeps raised from the strings not only the one damper but all the dampers, and many sympathetic harmonics arise from the freed strings. When the finger is the means employed to sustain the tone, but one damper is kept raised and the tone elicited is consequently very pure and clear and somewhat dry.

All good things are threefold, says the old proverb: in modern pianos there are usually three pedals, called respectGradual develop-ively First Pedal Damper Pedal, or simply Pedal; ment of modern Second, or Soft Pedal; Third,

Sostenuto or pedal usage Sustaining Pedal. The damper pedal is to the player's right side and when pressed raises the dampers collectively. The soft pedal is that on the left side. If one should ask: "Of what use are these pedals?" fifty out of a hundred music students and ninety-nine per cent of the laity would answer: "The one on the right is the loud pedal, and is used to make the music sound loud; the one on the left makes it soft. " But these are only rudimentary uses of the pedals, and are not even the most important ones. The term loud pedal, never correct, is not appropriate, for the damper pedal, although often used to strengthen the sound, has, besides, many other more important uses, one of which is its employment in connection with the soft pedal in pianissimo passages, to give the tone warmth and color.

It is true that when the art of piano-building was in its infancy the main service the damper pedal performed was to Primitive increase the volume of sound, for the tone of the damper pedal early pianos was so weak and evanescent that sympathetic vibration of all the strings was often needed. Thinness of harmony and dryness of melody would have resulted from a too frequent application of the dampers to the strings. Even as late as the early part of the nineteenth century all the dampers were often kept raised from the strings throughout many measures and regardless of the consequent blurring, in order to obtain sufficient tone.

Beethoven used the pedal freely in order to obtain the best effect of a tone-sustaining and songful legato. He told Czerny Beethoven's that ne nad once heard Mozart play the piano legato with the and that his touch was delicate, but that he had pedal a choppy style and no legato. This may have been on account of the action of the piano used by Mozart, which made strict legato impossible; but the remark gives us an idea of Beethoven's great fondness for legato in imitation of organ-effect, which Czerny says Beethoven seemed to produce in his playing.
Example 118

Beethoven — Largo, from C minor Concerto.

Czerny remarks in his correspondence with Cocks, a London publisher: "Legato in cantabile on the piano was at that time unknown, and Beethoven was the first to discover entirely new and impressive effects on that instrument." This new legato playing was produced with the pedal. We can have no doubt of this, as Czerny says that "Beethoven, in playing the Largo of his *C minor Concerto,* allowed the pedal to remain down throughout the whole theme. This could be done very well on the weak-sounding pianos of that time (1800), especially when the *una corda* pedal was also used. But now, as the tone of the modern piano has become much stronger, we should advise a renewed pressure of the pedal at every important change in the harmony, so that no defect may be noticeable in the sound." This use of the pedal in a cantabile passage played on our twentieth-century full-toned pianos would cause a blurring of the melody and a confusion of harmonies which would be a barbarous violation of good taste; but from what Czerny says we understand that in Beethoven's music, the pedal should be used as in other works, to sustain harmonies and to connect melodic tones without blurring them. This manner of playing is indispensable in cantabile passages and movements, if the intention of the composer be fulfilled. Besides the absolute legato required by the cantilena in this slow movement from the *Concerto, in C minor,* the effect to be imagined in the accompanying voices, regarding sustaining of tones (by means either of fingers or of pedal), is that of a string quartet or of an orchestra. The composer did not intend that more rests should be made than he has written down, and the enormous difficulty of connecting with the fingers all the tones of the different voices necessitates especial attention to this branch of piano playing, which is of much musical importance.

The marked improvement in the efficiency of the damping apparatus which was commonly used shortly after the period ow custom of of the composition of the *C minor Concerto* was using pedal once accompanied with a greater reserve in the use of in each measure e pedal. This became more and more necessary as the resonance of the piano increased, until, for those who used rules more than they did their ears, custom established the habit of renewing the pressure of the pedal with every measure, still, however, regardless of changes in harmony and dissonant tones in the melody.

The next step towards our modern standard of pedal usage was that mentioned by Czerny — to renew the pedal-pressure Greater reserve with every important harmonic change, although in use of pedal melodic purity was still disregarded. This way of playing was long continued, and numerous examples may be found even in modern editions of Field's Nocturnes, Heller's Etudes and thousands of other compositions in editions which but for the wrongly placed pedal-marks are good editions. For the notation endures to the present day, although no good player observes these marks as they are written. Apropos of this stage of development of pedal-usage are the pedal-marks in the following composition.

While it is largely due to the continually increasing sonority of the piano that pedal-marks which were once approximately satisfactory can no longer be relied upon Com,,sers. care. to assist the player, there is another prolific lessuse-ofpedaisource of incorrect pedal notation, which is, the marks exceeding labor and difficulty of indicating with accuracy the exact moment of pedal-attack and pedal-release. Rubinstein's solution of this problem was to rely upon the musicianship of the performer, and he therefore left his compositions as bare of all marks of expression as are those of Bach. Liszt, however, often indicated the use of the pedal, and always with exceeding power and nicety. Many more modern composers imitate him in this, notably Sgambati and Chaminade, but unhappily the majority of composers and editors, as well as engravers, are even in this latter day careless in their pedal notation.

Example 120
Mendelssohn — Song without Words, Op. 67, No. 1.

In Peters's edition of Mendelssohn's *Song without Words, in F major, Op.* 85, and in the one in *Eb, Op.* 67, the pedal is marked in such a manner that on a modern piano a faithful following of the marks would produce very bad effects of blurring the tones Dampers con-of the melody, many of which are foreign to the trolled by fingers harmony; but a more discreet use calculated to an pe a avoid such blurring can be adopted only in com bination with a well-thought-out sustaining of bass, upper bass and harmony tones. This can be done by substituting one finger for another on a key before allowing the key to rise, as described in connection with *Example* 124, thus sustaining as many tones as possible with the fingers, while the pedal is pressed and allowed to rise as often as is necessary to avoid blurring the melody. If this sustaining of all the tones of the harmony (suggested by the composer's pedal-marks) is not obtained, the effect is dry and fulness of harmony is sacrificed.

The above-mentioned manner is the only means to solve the hard problem which confronts the modern player in almost incorrectly every piece, namely, the necessity of sacrificing marked pedal neither the richness of harmony nor the clearness studies of melody. This leaves the composer or the editor so perplexed that he usually either marks the pedal entirely too much, and incorrectly, or not at all; so that in any case the player must have sufficient experience to divine the intention of the composer, and to treat the pedal, in combination with the touch, in such a way that the intended effect is satisfactorily produced. The best pianists of today, in playing cantabile passages, blur neither the melody nor the harmony, but manage, by a judicious use of the fingers as well as of the pedal, to render the harmony full and the melody pure. It is an astonishing fact that in the *Pedal Studies* of Schytte all the pedal-marks are wrongly placed. For instance, in the example given below, observance of the pedal-marks would disconnect the legato harmonies and render them staccato, while the melody tones would be staccato in some places and badly blurred in others, manifestly contrary to the intention of the composer. There are also several other collections of pedal studies by less distinguished musicians that have similar errors.

The management of the dampers in sustaining and connecting sound by means of the fingers alone should be mastered before attempting to control the dampers by The damper means of the pedal, the function of which is thus Pedal stated by Albino Gorno: "The correct use of the damper-pedal consists in controlling the dampers by means of the foot, so as to obtain certain desirable results which the fingers alone cannot produce."

Pedal effects are of two general classes: first, tone-sustaining and connecting; second, tone-coloring. Not only are there many poetic effects which the fingers cannot accomplish unaided, but the employment of the pedal is often imperative to the correct musical rendition. "All that can be taught," says Signor Gorno, "is merely correct usage. To speak of teaching an artistic use of the pedals is as unsuitable as it would be to speak of teaching an artistic use of chords, in the practical school of the harmony teacher."

It not infrequently happens that a tone should continue sounding for some time after it is necessary to remove the finger from the key which produced it, when of Management of course the finger can no longer be the tone-sus-dampers by taining medium. Instead, the foot becomes the finsersalone agent which keeps the damper raised by pressing down the damper-pedal before the finger is removed from the key-which is producing the tone; thus the string continues free to vibrate and emit sound so long as the pedal-pressure is maintained.

One of the aims of every pianist is the attaining of as good a legato as is compatible with the nature of his instrument, which, besides being somewhat short-toned, has the disadvantage

that every tone is produced by an attack of the hammer upon the strings, while true legato consists in the connection of unattacked tones. This true legato, of course, is impossible to obtain in piano-playing, yet it should be imitated. "He does not know how to connect two notes," was Chopin's severest censure of a pupil's playing. Legato in pianoforte playing consists in sustaining a tone until another tone is produced, so that connection of the two tones ensues, while the sound of the attack is minimized. All modern pianists are agreed that as a rule the pedal-pressure should be applied after the key is struck; this is sometimes called "after-pedaling," and sometimes, most incorrectly, is termed "syncopation of the pedal." If the pedal is applied simultaneously with the finger-stroke when it is desired to connect two tones of different pitch, the result is not a connection but an over-connection, a superlegato of the two tones which would both sound together contrary to the player's intention. In songful passages the pedal should not be pressed fully down, as this frees too many harmonics through the sympathetic vibration of the other strings and impairs purity of tone; a slight pressure is usually sufficient unless great volume of tone or long-sustained tone be required. The method of pressing the pedal will of course depend somewhat upon the length of the player's foot. To obtain the leverage necessary, either the ball of the foot or, if the player's foot be of insufficient length, the toes, should be placed quietly on the pedal before pressing it, so as to avoid the noise which would otherwise result from the sudden contact of foot with pedal. The foot should remain in full control of the pedal as it rises, and should not be suddenly removed, as the dampers falling abruptly on the strings and the pedal mechanism striking against its wooden support make sounds which annoy the hearer and distract his attention from the music being played. Neither should the pedal remove the dampers violently from the strings, as this sets them slightly in motion and their vibration causes an indefinite, rolling noise. "You beat

the drum," was a master's whimsical rebuke to a pupil who was guilty of these faults in pedaling.

The use of the damper-pedal (first pedal) is often essential to connect tones or chords so distant from each other that, although marked legato, the fingers necessarily Pedalusedt0 play them staccato. In the following example destroy fingerit is impossible to connect the slurred legato rests chords by means of the fingers, as unwritten and undesired rests occur when the fingers are removed from one key to another, causing a break in the continuity of sound undesired by the composer. When the pedal is properly used these undesired rests are obliterated and the chords are connected.

Example 122
Gorno — Material for the Study of the Pianoforte Pedals, Part I, No. 4.

The player should listen attentively in order to produce and to perceive strict connection of tone. If the fingers be taken away from the keys before the pedal is pressed down a disconnection of tone results, while if the pedal be held too long a blurring of one chord with another follows. In beginning the study of the damper-pedal it is best to be very exact in its use and to press the pedal down at a precise moment previously determined upon. This is indicated below the music upon the single line marked *Ped. C*, meaning *Pedal-line, 4/4 measure*. The notes and rests on this pedal-line indicate when the pedal should be pressed down and when allowed to rise. The measure should be counted aloud, 1, 2, 3, 4, and these figures written above the pedal-line help to show most definitely the moment of pedal pressure, which in this exercise occurs on the third beat of each measure. The chord played by the fingers on the first beat of the first measure is sustained through the third and the fourth beat by the pedal; therefore, immediately after the third beat, the fingers are not needed to sustain the tone and can be removed from the keys and placed upon the keys of the next chord, so as to be prepared to play it on the first beat. As soon as this prepared chord in the second measure is heard, connection of the two chords is made and the pedal should be released so as to avoid blurring them. The slow tempo in which this study first should be played allows plenty of time for the ear to make sure that the chord is sounding and that but one chord is sustained by pedal-pressure. Besides the graphic signs of pedalusage indicated by the notes and rests on the pedal-line the customary rather vague signs of *Ped.* and ® are written above the music — correctly.

It is often impossible to sustain the full harmony with the fingers alone, especially when it is in the form

Tones of wide-& ’.*J.* spread harmony of wide-spread arpeggiated harmonies such as are sustained by characteristic of the works of Chopin, Schumann pedal and Liszt, in which case the pedal is the only means of producing the superlegato required.

In *Example* 123 the pedal should be pressed directly after the bass-note is struck, so as to sustain it and all succeeding tones of the same harmony; as soon as the bass-tone Ab is connected to the next bass-tone in the succeeding harmony, the pedal should be released, as indicated by the eighth-rest; then, while the bass-tone is held by means of the fingers, the pedal should be pressed down on the second eighth of the second measure, so as to sustain this new bass-tone and the harmony founded upon it. As before, the moments of pedal-pressure and of pedal-release are defined with nicety by means of the rests and notes on the pedal-line.

A judicious fingering has much to do with a correct use of the pedal. It frequently happens that bass and inner voices should be sustained, yet that the purity of the Weii-thoughtmelodic tones should not be marred by the great out fingering number of overtones which form in continually gatory increasing numbers from the moment when a tone is held by the pedal until the pedal is released by the foot. In cantabile passages it is often best to hold these accompanying tones with the fingers until the moment when they are obliged to release the keys, thereby delaying the use of the pedal.

In this orchestral passage from Liszt's transcription of one of Chopin's songs it is necessary to sustain tones of the arpeggiated harmony in the left hand and also to use the pedal afresh with each tone of the melody in the right hand. An unblurred melody accompanied by a sustained bass and accomshiftin. panying full harmony may be obtained by com fingers upon a bining pedal effect of sustained tone produced by ey means of the foot with the pedal effect of sustained tone produced by means of the fingers. The fifth finger should be substituted swiftly for the thumb on the second and fourth keys struck with the left hand, so as to sustain longer the upper bass-tones and following tones by means of the fingers. In the second measure the fourth finger is similarly shifted upon the second and fourth keys struck. Such substitution of one finger for another is a very useful device continually and almost involuntarily applied by good players to sustain tone and at the same time to prepare the fingers to produce other tones. The Mendelssohn *Song without Words, in E, Example* 120, can only be played by a similar substitution of one finger for another.

X, When solid chords are connected, this shifting of the fingers often takes place simultaneously in several voices at once, as is shown in *Example* 125, which gives comparatively simple material for practice of this very necessary form of finger technic. At the beginning of the study the fingers alone make the connection of tone and the crescendo, and towards the close the power of tone is augmented from f to *ff* and the quality of tone changed by the use of the pedal.

A shifting fingering is very suitable for the left hand in the closing measures of Debussy's *Arabesque, in E major.* The fingering in the right hand greatly facilitates the playing on account of the desirable inward inclination of the wrist which it necessitates. The tones sustained by the left hand make possible skilled and sufficiently frequent slight pressures of the pedal.’

In his studies from Caprices by Paganini, Schumann indicates a simulta-

neous shifting of two fingers in chord connection similar to that in *Example* 125, and gives many Schumann's instances of a single shift upon one key. He says: fingering "The editor further calls attention to the silent substitution of fingers on a single key, which often makes a fine effect, and to the wide arpeggios of the left hand, requiring a wise use of the pedal, which is intrusted to the thoughtful player. He has indicated a very exact and carefully thought out fingering as the fundamental basis of an able performance. The student should therefore above all pay attention to this. If, however, the playing is also to be technically fine he should strive for swing and softness of tone, for rounding and precision of the separate parts, and for flow and lightness of the whole. Then after overcoming all external difficulties the fantasy will be able to move safely and sportively and to give life, light and shade and easily to complete whatever else might be lacking to a freer presentation of the work. The examples here given are intended only to call attention to similar ones The editor even advises advanced players to practise but seldom exercises from Methods for the Piano, but rather to invent their own.... In No. 5,1 intentionally omitted all signs of delivery, that the student might search the heights and depths for himself. For testing the pupil's conceptional faculty this procedure would seem very well adapted." Example 127

Schumann — Papillons, Op. 2, No. 12.

Schumann gives examples to illustrate the quick releasing, 0neof one by one, of the tones of the harmony, by a

Schumann's method which he also employs in the final cadence devu:cs of the *Papillons,* shown in *Example* 127, and at the close of the *Grandfather's Dance.*

Although he does not in any way indicate it on the printed page, Paderewski employs this manner of playing the Cadenza PaderewskTs of his own *Minuet a I 'antique,* in order to enrich *m&c* and beautify the tone *D* which reintroduces the original theme. Out from the harmony it floats, an ethereal, singing tone magically born,of the sound-waves, captivating the hearer yet mystifying him as to the means employed to produce a voice so exquisitely fine yet full.

Example 129

Gorno — Pedal Studies, Part II, No. 42. Another valuable expedient is the substitution of a finger of one hand for a finger of the other hand. In the above exercise the melody-tones, Db and Gb, can only be held substitution of for their indicated duration of a measure and a one finger for half by the substitution of the fifth finger of the reieasing the right hand for the second finger of the left hand, tones as indicated by the fingering and the abbreviations *m.s.* (left hand) and *m.d.* (right hand).

The Gorno etude is in the nature of a preparatory study for such passages as the closing measures of Chopin's *F major Nocturne, Op.* 15, which should be played in a similar manner, in order to sustain the melody-tone *G* into the next measure until *F* is produced, while at the same time sustaining the bass and all the other tones of the arpeggiated harmony.

Often, as in the above study, the pedal must be used to preserve the legato of the melody. The notes on the two lower staves are the ones played and, in combination with the signs on the pedal-line below, represent the manner of execution. The notes on the highest staff show the cantabile effect to be imagined and produced. This connection of melody is somewhat difficult because of the repetitions of the melodic tones in the accompanying voices. The pedal is used to connect the melody-tones and also to make superlegato harmony. Almost more important is the management of the fingers so as to obtain the quality of attack desired. These effects should also be practised without the pedal, the player obtaining the legato and the superlegato as well as possible with the fingers alone, by allowing the keys which produce the melodic tones to rise only about half-way before depressing them again for the production of the repeated *pp* accompanying tones of the same pitch. To produce the sustained accom-panying tones without breaking the legato of the melody it is necessary for the keys not to rise to the level of the keyboard, but to be depressed only from the height at which they feel the resistance and the weight of the key, as previously described in connection with the figure on page 160. Etudes 28-32 of the Gorno *Material for the Study of the Pianoforte Pedals* give varieties of studies of melody notes repeated in the accompaniment and sustained by the pedal. The tonesustaining by the fingers, as described, is very necessary in such compositions as the slow movement of Beethoven's *C minor Sonata, Op.* 13, which may be conceived as a piece written for strings, and should therefore be played with great purity of tone and but little resort to the pedal. Usually accompanying tones such as those in *Example* 2 and in the Haydn and the Mozart Sonatas should be sustained by the fingers alone and in this manner; and great skill in this touch is required in playing most of the examples in Chapters X and XI.

It has been shown that the term "loud pedal" is inadequate to suggest the various functions of the important piece of mechanism frequently so called. The term "soft pedal" is also somewhat of a misnomer, for this pedal may be used to modify the tone-coloring when playing loud passages. Still, this is the name customarily applied to it. The mechanism of this pedal varies with the form of piano to which it is attached. In the now almost disused square piano the soft pedal muffles the strings by inserting a piece of felt between them and the hammers. In Beethoven's time this pedal was called the celeste. A form of it is still to be found in upright pianos, where the middle pedal is often a "practice pedal" or muffling pedal. The action of the soft pedal in the upright piano usually consists in moving the hammers closer to the strings so that the blow is shortened. This kind of pedal used to be called the *Pedale d'expression.* In the grand piano, pressure upon the soft pedal shifts the hammers slightly to the right (or, rarely, to the left), so that the number of unison strings which receives the blow of each hammer is diminished by one, although the unstruck string vibrates sympathetically, enriching while changing the tonal quality by means of its unattacked tone. Of this the modern pianist takes advantage in order to produce the greatest possible changes in tone-qualities. The pressure exerted on the soft pedal usually should be sufficient to force it quickly down to its utmost limit, otherwise an undesired metallic sound may be produced when the strings receive the blow from the sides of the grooves made by them in the felt of the hammers. In consequence of the nature of its mechanism the soft pedal must be depressed before producing the tones to be affected by it.

Apropos of his performance of some Haydn compositions, Rubinstein, at one of his Historical Lecture-Recitals, commented Rubinstein's use thus upon his use of the soft pedal: "I have of the soft pedal played all of his music to you with my foot upon the left pedal. In my opinion the tone of the modern pianoforte is too powerful to present aright the music of his epoch."

The soft pedal is employed both alone and in combination with the other pedals to gain variety of tone coloring, and it serves in the production of echo-like effects in repeating a phrase which previously has been played rather loud.

Echo effect

When this pedal is employed in connection with the damperpedal the echo seems mysteriously veiled, as though coming through a haze from a distance. In the above Gorno study the full harmony is sustained in the second measure mainly by the damper-pedal; in the third measure the repeated notes, *quasi eco* (like an echo), are played while both the pedals are pressed down. The second pedal *Ped.* 2) greatly assists in obtaining the echo effect.

Hans Schmitt says that the great artist Franz Liszt used the soft pedal felicitously to heighten the beauty of the arpeggios in his *Spinning Song* transcribed from *The Flying Dutchman.* He first played the arpeggio fortissimo; then, without raising his foot from the damper-pedal, and using also the soft pedal, he repeated the arpeggio pianissimo and somewhat more slowly. This gives the repeated passage the entrancing effect of floating in nebulous sound.

Liszt's pedaling

The third pedal

Placed between the soft pedal and the damper-pedal is the sostenuto pedal. Its proper function is to sustain one tone or a single chord to the exclusion of all others. There are, however, two kinds of third pedal, one of which is of little value, since it is merely a partial damperpedal controlling the dampers of the strings of the lowest octaves only; while the damper-pedal removes the damper from all the strings excepting those of a variable number of keys — about twenty — in the highest register of the piano, which have no dampers. This kind of so-called sostenuto pedal is unsatisfactory, as it is merely a partial damper-pedal, for while any string struck in the lower octaves may be made free of the dampers, so also are all the dampers of the entire lower range of the piano, thus allowing all the strings of the entire division controlled by the third pedal to vibrate in sympathy with each other and with all the other strings whose dampers are raised by the fingers in the upper and the middle parts of the piano, producing an effect of blurring very nearly as bad as when the principal damper-pedal (first pedal) is in use.

But the use of the true sostenuto pedal produces no effect of blurring, as it is not a partial damper-pedal, since it has no True sostenuto power to raise the dampers; it merely keeps pedal raised such dampers, one or many, as are raised at the moment this pedal is put down. As long as the foot maintains its pressure on the third pedal the tone of the sounding string whose damper is kept raised by a pressure on the third pedal will continue until it dies gradually away; but at any time the tone may be renewed by a fresh finger stroke. When the pedal pressure is removed the damper again falls upon the string, stops its vibration, and the sound ceases. This variety of third pedal has no effect on tones produced *after* it is put down, as

it holds up the dampers which are raised the moment it is pressed down, and no others.

This kind of pedal is considered a very ingenious and artistically valuable piece of mechanism by modern players and Liszt's deli ht in musical thinkers who have weighed the many the sostenuto advantages which can be derived from its use. pedal This *Pedale de prolongement,* or *Debain's prolong ment,* as it was variously called, was bought and improved by Theodore Steinway and applied to his piano in 1874. Strange to say, although the patent expired some years ago, and many American pianos are now using it (with success varying in proportion to the sonority of the instrument), it is even now but little known in Europe. Yet so great was Liszt's delight in it that he wrote to Steinway: "I can only sit and admire the wonderful results in tone, strength and completeness of this new instrument. That you may have an example of what can now be done with the piano since your wonderful sostenuto pedal permits the longer sustaining of tones, I send you two examples — one the *Dance of Sylphs* of Berlioz and the other No. 3 of my *Consolation.* Today I wrote the opening measures of these arrangements as they can now be played since you have added this pedal to the piano. If you wish it, I will with pleasure rewrite the whole transcription with special view to this wonderful addition to the piano."

In many other pieces we find passages, either long or short, which would almost seem to have been composed intending the use of the sostenuto pedal. Such sustained pedal-is the case in many measures of the Introduction JTMm4 to the *Rondo, in lb,* by Chopin, in *Example* 135, where the CF in octave should be sustained as a pedal-point with the third pedal while in the middle and upper part of the piano the hands play passages comprising many tones which do not belong to the harmony with which they are played.

In order to sustain the Cb, the composer himself marks the pedal as held down continually. But by employing the

third pedal to hold up the two dampers from the strings sounding Cb, and from these strings only, the tone can be sustained according to the composer's intention without blurring the harmonies; then later, the damper-pedal can also be employed to advantage for the general effect.

Example 136

Bach — C Minor Prelude, from The Well-tempered Clavichord.

The eminent player and Bach scholar, Busoni, in his edition of *The Well-tempered Clavichord,* points out some of the advanThird pedal an tages of the sostenuto pedal. He says of the 28th aid in Bach-measure of the *Prelude in C minor* in the first part of that work: "The artist must know, among playing other things, how to husband his strength for climaxes and turning points, and how to seize opportunities for gathering new strength. This consideration makes the addition of a hold over *G* in the left hand appear justifiable; it should lend to the bass a certain organ-like ponderousness, and throw the Presto — 'bearing down all barriers' with its irresistible flood — into a yet stronger relief; the point of rest thus gained before this *quasi cadenza* will enable the player to recover the necessary lightness and elasticity which are apt to suffer from twenty-four measures of an obstinately monotonous movement. Finally, this same left-hand *G* may be transformed, by adding the lower octave and employing the Steinway third pedal *(pidale de prolongement,* or sustaining pedal), into an effective sixmeasure organ point."

Similar passages where the third pedal is of effective aid occur in hundreds of compositions, among which may be named Bach's *Organ Fantasie, in C minor,* Saint-Saens' *G minor Concerto,* Chopin's *Prelude, in Af* and his *F# minor Nocturne* (second part), Schumann's *Papillons, Op. 2, No. 12.* In simultaneous many cases all three pedals can be used together use of ail three advantageously. Often, as in Liszt's *Venezia* pedals *e Napoli* this is almost a necessity, in order to obtain the best color effect. While the fingers on the keys and the right foot on the damper-pedal are correctly used to sustain and connect tone, the left foot, if of sufficient length and breadth, should press simultaneously the soft pedal and the sostenuto pedal. For the pianist with a small foot there remains but the hope that some enterprising piano-builder will make it possible to lock the soft pedal after pressing it down (as can be done with the practice-pedal sometimes found in cheap pianos) or in some other way make it easy for the pianist to use all three pedals simultaneously.

Example 137

Bach — Musette from English Suite, in D minor.

3d Rsd

Venino, in his *Pedal Method,* says of the *Gavotte and Musette* in the *English Suite, in D minor,* that "the trio (played *una corda* and pianissimo) is another example wherein the damper-pedal can be used from beginning to end without change. Instead of detracting from the piece, the pedal thus applied rather heightens the effect. The entire part rests upon an organpoint *D* in the bass, and is in imitation of a Bagpipe (Musette)." However, this effect of drone-bass can be produced much better with the sostenuto pedal, which should be used so as to sustain the final bass oct

Third pedal sometimes preferable to damperpedal than musical content

Regarding this desirable sounding of certain tones over their apparent duration as indicated by the notes, Billow says of measures 19-22 of the second part of the second more important movement of the *Sonata, Op.* 101: "The composer's direction to make the organ-point *Db* sound on audibly through four measures has the disadvantage, it is true, of confusing the effect of the parts in canon, but here, as often elsewhere, secondary considerations must be sacrificed to essentials — the latter being the sensuous tonal effect." The conservative Reinecke agrees with him on this point, and says: "These bars will sound somewhat indistinct and vague, as Beethoven requires the raising of the dampers through all four bars, in order that the low *D* may continue sounding

as a pedal-point. This confusion of sound can be somewhat lessened if during the first two bars one plays the two upper parts with one hand (provided that the stretching capacity of the right hand admits of it) and holds down the Db (on the other hand) uninterruptedly with a finger of the left hand, and now lets the dampers fall again more often. " Comparatively few hands are capable of the great extension required in following Reinecke's suggested manner of performance; but it is an easy matter to play these measures so as to sustain the pedal-point without blurring the imitations if, instead of using the damper-pedal as indicated by Beethoven with the signs *Ped.* and , the third pedal be employed as indicated in the above example.

It is interesting and useful to note the meaning of the terms *con sordino* and *senza sordino* which Beethoven has employed so often in his earlier compositions and especially Con sordino in his first three Concertos, as can be seen in those With dampers. old editions which are in accordance with the Wlthout pedal original manuscripts and in the Franz Kullak edition published by Steingraber. *Sordino* is an Italian word which is very often misunderstood, as it has two meanings. The *sordino* for the violinist is the mute, but in piano music the word means damper. Consequently *con sordino* means with dampers, that is, without pedal; *senza sordino* means without dampers, that is, with pedal.

Beethoven adopted this manner of expressing himself in indicating the use of the dampers, because at the time of composing these Concertos (1795-1800) the cloven Hand stops, foot-pedal was of comparatively recent invention faee-pedai (Broadwood, 1783) and was not in general use; instead, hand stops (invented about 1760) were used to operate the damping apparatus in either or both of two sections, bass and treble, and a little later, especially in Germany, the dampers were raised by means of a divided knee-pedal *(genouillieres),* which could be employed to raise the dampers in two sections, treble and bass, or to raise all the dampers simul-

taneously. The knee-pedal remained in use until about 1830. "The machine pressed by the knee," writes Mozart to his father in 1777, "is prompt to raise the dampers, or, on discontinuing the pressure ever so little, is as prompt to let them down upon the strings again, when not the least after-resonance is heard." In the *C minor Concerto (Example* 118) the words *con sordino* and *senza sordino,* which call for the use and disuse of the dampers, are frequently used, and give a very clear idea of the composer's desire regarding the use of the dampers and the effects deriving from their use. Throughout the *Largo* these terms are used very often, sometimes in reference to a passage and sometimes to one note only, showing that Beethoven used the pedal intuitively and according to the best modern usage. In the sixty-two measures of solo in this movement he employs *con sordino* twenty-one times and *senza sordino* nineteen times. In his Bl, *Concerto* he uses the term *con sordino ad libitum.*

The London *Musical Times* of August 1, 1895, contains an article by J. S. Shedlock on *Beethoven and the Sordino.* The paper is written in refutation of a previous one which stated that the *sordini* of the piano consisted of that apparatus of felt or leather which muffles the tone when inserted between the hammers and strings, the effect being similar to that produced by the soft pedal of our modern square pianos. The author says: "Carl Czerny, who was a pupil of Beethoven, said in his *Pianoforte School,* Vol. 4, that he studied many of Beethoven's works under the master's own guidance and enjoyed his friendly and instructive intercourse and that he had been asked to treat, in the School, of the performance of Beethoven's works. The volume is made up chiefly of suggestions on the proper performance of all Beethoven's works for piano solo, including metronome marks, giving the time in which Beethoven himself performed his works, and very full instructions for the use of the pedal — as he calls it, *in any case,* the damper, loud or right-foot pedal. One sentence says that Beethoven employed the pedal much more frequently than we find it indicated in his compositions. In his remarks on *Op. 26, Var.* 5, Czerny says: 'The last fifteen bars, *senza sordino,'* that is, with the pedal, as it was indicated at the period when this sonata appeared. To the *Sonata, in C# minor, Op. 27,* he gives the direction *lsempre sordino,'* explaining this by 'the prescribed pedal must be employed with each note of the bass. ' Further he directs when the pianissimo pedal is to be used and where it is not to be used in conjunction with the *senza sordino* or damper-pedal in the way he prescribes. In the third movement, *Presto Agitato,* he says that with the fortissimo quaver chords, at the end of bar two of this movement, and whenever they occur, the pedal must always be used. In the suggestion as to the playing of the *Rondo, Op.* 53, he says: 'This Rondo, of a pastoral character, is entirely calculated for the use of the pedal which is here actually expressed.' And in a footnote to this same sentence he adds: 'The indication *senza sordino* was only continued as long as the pedal was pressed with the knee.' Czerny never speaks of a pianissimo pedal (leather and felt, interposed between hammers and strings) called *sordino.* He does say that there were pedals other than the two now used, but that they were soon discarded, all others being acknowledged as unworthy of the true artist. His pianissimo pedal is the shifting pedal. *Senza sordino,* with him, is a pedal pressed by the knee, by which the dampers are raised, and is an earlier indication for producing the effect later on and now obtained by means of the pedal. *Con sordino* is the opposite of this, and equals . Czerny ought to know what he is talking about. He himself is sure of the correctness of his remarks, and claims, in a concluding paragraph to the solo sonatas, that his remarks are correct. If he is any authority in pianoforte matters and Beethoven in particular, the above should be of value." /What Czerny has said of the matter is important because, having been a pupil of Beethoven and having studied his Sonatas with the composer himself, Czerny undoubtedly acquired a correct idea of Beethoven's desire regarding the use both of soft and of damper pedals, and clearly understood what the composer meant by his manner of indicating the use of the *sordini* (dampers) of the piano, as well as of the *una cor da* pedal. But even without the above statement of Czerny's the same conclusions are reached by looking over the earlier compositions of Beethoven in those old editions which employ the above expressions to indicate the damper and soft pedals and in the edition published by Breitkopf & Hartel which preserves the original text. By *senza sordino* Beethoven undoubtedly meant with pedal, as this marking is found in forte and fortissimo passages, an effect which would have been impossible with the muffling pedal *celeste)* which greatly diminished the tone.

Liszt also interprets *senza sordino* as equivalent to the use of the damper-pedal, as is shown in his edition of the first three Concertos, and it is noteworthy that he has not found it necessary to change any of the pedal-marks, although he makes some additional ones, indicating them in small characters while the original signs are of the usual size. The pedal was used by Beethoven to produce the effect of increasing the intensity of tone, of sustaining many tones that could not be sustained by Liszt's edition of ne frng61"8, and all other effects which for musical Beethoven's reasons are produced by the modern pianist. Of concertos course Beethoven was desirous of obtaining color by means of the pedals in order that the passage might express his meaning, not merely for the sake of tone-coloring as it might be applied in piano-music that is more brilliant and wellsounding than deep in thought and feeling.

Not only was the damper-pedal preceded by stops. The soft pedal, also (the shifting pedal of our grand pianos), was preuna corda. ceded by two shifting hand-stops. In Beethoven's

Due corde time, as in ours, finger-pressure upon a key in the upper or the middle register of the piano caused a damper to rise from three unison strings and a hammer to strike them. The hand-stops enabled the player to shift the action so that each hammer instead of striking three unison strings would strike either two unison strings *(due corde)* or one string *(una corda).* The disuse of these stops, permitting the hammer again to strike three unison strings, was called for by the expression *tre corde* (three strings) and *tutte le corde* (all the strings). Sometimes the *una corda* stop and the *due corde* stop were separate mechanisms, and sometimes one stop effected the two different shifts of the hammers. These piano and pianissimo stops were invented by Stein in Vienna in 1789, and they were long considered indispensable parts of the piano. Beethoven indicates their use in some of his finest compositions. In the slow movement of the great *G major Concerto,* composed in 1806, he indicates the use of the damper-pedal in the usual modern way. But to obtain the expression which this wonderful piece of music requires the soft pedal as well as the damper-pedal must be employed to obtain an effect as nearly as possible in accordance with the composer's directions as expressed in the following French words placed at the beginning of the *Largo: Dans tout cet Andante on tient levee la Pedale, qui ne fait sonner qu'une corde. ' An signe Ped. on line, outre cela les etouffoirs.* (All through this Andante use the pedal which makes only one string sound. At the sign *Ped.* raise the dampers besides.) After having directed the use of the *una corda* stop to diminish the tone, towards the end of the movement he uses the following expression: *2 et puis 3 cordes,* meaning employ first two strings and then three strings. He demands at the same time *crescendo sino al fortissimo* (increasing to fortissimo), and after a few measures of fortissimo he adds, *2 et puis 1 corde* (two strings and then one), in combination with *dim. sino al pianissimo* (decrease to pianissimo).

Beethoven prescribes the use of the pedals minutely and accurately in some of his most important works. In the slow movement of his *Sonata, in B, Op.* 106, he calls Tutte le corde for the effects of *una corda* (one string), *due corde Tutto a cembalo,* (two strings) and *tre corde* (three strings) with M,temerSaite continued alternation throughout the piece. The *una corda* called for in the first measure lasts until the twenty-seventh measure, when *tutte le corde* takes its place and governs the playing of the next thirty measures; then, in quick succession, sometimes following each other at intervals of a measure only, *una corda* is employed five times, followed three times by the usual *tutte le corde,* and twice by *poco a poco due e allora tutte le corde* (little by little two and then all the strings). Towards the end of the piece *una corda* followed by *tutte le corde* is used five times. Beethoven's use of these signs both in quick succession and also at long intervals apart, as in this piece, shows his desire for varied tone-color and also his carefulness in writing the signs exactly as he wished them to be placed. Sometimes he employs the Italian expression *poco a poco tutte le corde* (little by little all the strings), meaning that the performer should pass gradually from the use of one string to the use of all the strings by means of the stops, and *poco a poco due e allora tutte le corde* (little by little two and then all the strings). In the slow movement of Op. 101 he employs the German, expressions: *Mit einer Saite* (with one string), *Nach und nach mehrere Saiten* (gradually all the strings), *Alle Saiten* (all the strings) and the Italian words *Tutto il cembalo ma piano* (all the piano but softly).

Mendelssohn also employs *una corda* and *tutte le corde* quite frequently in his pianoforte compositions. In the first movement of his *Sonata, in E major, Op.* 6, written in 1826, Mendelssohn's ne uses ne following expressions: *una corda pp* use of una *dolce, tutte le corde, una corda pp e dolce, espressivo* cmda *p e sempre una corda, pp tutte le corde.* Some what similar expressions are employed in the third movement of this same sonata, in the third *Caprice, Op.* 33, and in the Scherzo of the *Sonata, Op.* 106. Even nowadays these terms are frequently employed, although the mechanism of the damping and shifting apparatus is greatly altered from that of earlier days.

Schumann's notation of the soft pedal consists in the use of the German word *Verschiebung.* As an example, in the first Mit verschie-measure of the Allegro from his *Concerto, Op.* 134, bung: with soft occur the words *mit Verschiebung* (with shifting pe pedal), and four measures later he indicates its disuse by the words *ohne Verschiebung* (without shifting pedal).

i While examination of Beethoven's music shows that he availed himself to the full of the coloring powers of the pedals Moscheies' use of his day, it is equally evident that other good of the pedals musicians and fine pianists who did not possess his genius seem to have been without his fine perception of their color-value. Moscheles, although twenty-four years younger than Beethoven, and therefore playing a more modern piano than he, writes in the following strain: "It is my duty to show that such a thing as a pianissimo can be obtained without the soft pedal. The pedals are auxiliaries; whoever makes them of primary importance puts in evidence the incapacity of his own fingers." "I can slowly spin out the tone as upon a stringed instrument, and that, too, without using the soft pedal; as for the soft pedal I do not require it to produce a pianissimo, and can rely solely upon touch." "A good pianist uses the pedals as little as possible; too frequent use easily leads to abuse. Moreover, why should he try to produce an effect with his feet instead of his hands?" "A good player must only rarely use the assistance of either pedal, otherwise he misuses it." "I wish he had not his feet so perpetually upon the pedals. All effects now it seems must be produced by the feet — what is the good of people having hands? It is just as if a good rider wanted forever to use spurs." Of Thalberg, Moscheles wrote: "Thalberg plays famously, but he is not my man.... He plays forte and piano with the pedals but not with the hand."

Born within a few years of Chopin, Schumann, Mendelssohn and Liszt, Thalberg did much to popularize the use of the pedals as color media. He writes in *L'Art du* Thalberg, *Chant:* "In the use of the pedals, which play so Marmontei important a part in execution, we should take the greatest care never to mix dissimilar harmonies and thus produce disagreeable dissonances. There are pianists who make such an abuse of the pedals, or rather they use them with so little logic, that their sense of hearing is perverted and they have lost their appreciation of pure harmony." In a somewhat similar strain Marmontel writes: "The greatest number of pupils to whom the use of the pedal is permitted, make use of it to beat the time, or better, to put it down and never let it go. This produces a frightful cacophony, to the affliction of all musicians of taste." These sayings show the gradual development of pedal usage and the growing appreciation, by the fine pianist, of the pedal, which Venino calls "the life-giving power to the pianist, that which vitalizes a composition as the sunlight vitalizes dormant colors, or the breath the human body." They also indicate the barbarous use to which, in the past as in the present, ordinary pianists put the pedals, the difficulty of teaching their correct use, and their rise, in the esteem of pianists, from the humble position of "auxiliary" to the exalted one of "soul" of the pianoforte.

The finest and most crystallized expression upon this subject which has found its way into print since that of Rubinstein, comes from the pen of Josef Hofmann, in josef Hofmann his *Piano Playing.* "As the eye guides the fingers on the pedals when we read music, so must the ear be the guide — and the 'sole' guide.— of the foot upon the pedal. The foot is merely the servant, the executive agent, while the ear is the guide, the judge, and the final criterion. If there is any phase in pianoplaying where we should remember particularly that music is for the ear, it is in the treatment of the pedal.... It should be remembered that the pedal is not merely the means of tone prolongation but also a means of coloring — and preeminently that. What is generally understood by the term 'piano-charm' is to the greatest extent produced by an artistic use of the pedal. The moment when the blending of non-harmonic tones imperils the tonal beauty of the piece in hand can be determined solely and exclusively by the player's own ear, and here we are once more at the point from which this article started, namely: that the ear is governor, and that it alone can decide whether or not there is to be any pedal.... We should, therefore, endeavor to train the susceptibility of our ear, and we should ever make it more difficult to gain the assent of our own ear than to gain that of our auditors.... To hear ourselves play — that is, to listen to our own playing — is the bed-rock basis of the technique of the pedal.... Now, as the right pedal should not be used to cover a lack of force, so should the left pedal not be regarded as a license to neglect the formation of a fine *pianissimo* touch. It should not cloak or screen a defective *pianissimo*, but should serve exclusively as a means of coloring where the softness of tone is coupled with what the jewelers call 'dull finish.' For the left pedal does not soften the tone without changing its character; it lessens the quantity of tone but at the same time it also markedly affects the quality.... Train your ear and then use both pedals honestly!"

Reference has been made to the fact that not only is it often desirable and frequently imperative for certain tones to continue sounding longer than is indicated by the value of their notes, but this desirable sounding of tones over their apparent duration should often be extended through written rests, as in *Example* 117.

It is not always an easy matter to decide whether the composer has intended rests of silence or sounding rests, although the composer's desire to have his music interpreted exactly as he conceived it is sometimes so strong as to lead him to employ unusual notation for the purpose. Carl Reinecke, in his letters on the Beethoven Pianoforte Sonatas, referring to the *Rondo* of the *Sonata*, Op. 53, dedicated to Waldstein, makes the following pregnant remarks concerning the rests Beethoven.s in the few measures before the *Prestissimo* in peculiar notation the last movement: "No one seems to have un-ofrests derstood for what reason Beethoven cut up the bar-rest into two quarter-rests. And yet it is so easy. That is to say, it would have been impossible to indicate in any other way the exact letting down of the dampers with the entry of the second quarter-rest. An analogous case is in the second movement of his *G major Concerto*, where he has cut up an eighth-rest into two sixteenths." The measures referred to are given in the following example.

Example 140
Beethoven — G Major Concerto, Rondo.
If
Notes prolonged throughout many measures in which rests occur are found in Beethoven's *Sonata, in F minor, Op. 57*, where the composer has marked not only Ped.,but also frequently uses *sempre peddle* (always pedal).
Sempre pedale Example 141
Beethoven — Sonata, in F minor, Op. 57.

The expression *sempre pedale* does not mean that the player is to keep the pedal pressed down continuously, but to continue to use the pedal freely so as to bring out the effect desired by the composer. The word *Ped.* used alone and not followed by a star has the same meaning as *sempre pedale* and is often used to indicate the desirability of sustaining a pedal-point or certain other tones (most frequently in the bass) without too much blurring of the other voices. The sign of a star for pedal release is omitted because, as the proper use of the pedal cannot clearly be indicated by signs, its discriminative employment is left to the judgment of the performer.

Most modern composers employ this method, among others, to indicate the use of the pedal. For example, Sgambati, in his s ambati's *Toccata, in Ab, Op. 18, No. 4*, indicates the neces pedal sary sustaining of a double pedal-point through
"na"o" many measures, placing the word *Ped.* under the notes *F* and *C* written as eighth-notes, and using no sign of pedal release, although seven measures later he again uses the word *Pedal*. This points out the composer's desire for the sustained pedal-point without a disagreeable blurring of the notes of the passage played above it. That Sgambati is very careful in his use of the pedal is shown frequently in his published works. On the first three pages of the *Etude de Concert, in F#, Op. 10*, he uses both *Ped.* and *#*, and *Ped.* without the star; then for a page and a half he employs Kohler's pedal notation— notes and rests on a single pedal-line; after which he returns to his former notation.

In Mendelssohn's works the words *sempre pedale* are usually followed sooner or later by *#*. This is often as confusing as when no sign whatever is given to drop the Mendelssohn's dampers. Even Schmitt, with his extensive and pedal notation accurate knowledge of the pedal, fails in one instance to appreciate the true value of the *sempre pedale*, for after having discussed it at some length and apparently with full understanding of its meaning, he says of the passage given in *Example* 120: "It may be more positively asserted that the *sempre pedale* at the conclusion of the sixth Song without Words is not intended to be observed as there indicated; Mendelssohn certainly never wished it to be played as he wrote it." But it is evident from the explanation just given and from the text in conjunction with *Example* 120 that Mendelssohn did intend the words *sempre pedale* to be observed as he there indicated; but of course his words are not to be understood according to the letter merely, but in the spirit in which they were written, and as they are meant by all good composers. This also applies to the Chopin *Example* 107. Of all the notation used in pianoforte music that intended for the pedal is the most inadequate, contradictory and puzzling, except to the musician-pianist, to whom all is plain, and excepting, also, those unthinking, unhearing players who say: "I tell my pupils just to obey the signs; to put down the pedal when it is marked and to let it up when they see the star, and not to use it at all unless the sign is written in the music."

At the beginning of a composition Schumann often employs the words *Pedal, Paddle,* or *Mit Pedal,* — whether or not followed by sign of pedal release, — with the significance of Mit Pedal *sempre pedale.* The terms *pedal* and *pedale*

Pedaie grande. he uses with exceeding frequency throughPedaietenuto ou. go many compositions that it would be a simpler matter to designate those pieces in which he does not employ these signs than those in which they do occur. He likewise uses the terms *col pedale* (always with pedal), *sempre tenuto per il pedale* (always held with the pedal) and *pedale grande.*

When the use of the pedal is necessary for harmonic reasons, and the melody moves rather rapidly, there is great danger that Senza pedaie. the melody will be blurred unless the fingers have senza tempo learned to sustain tone properly. With this in mind, the composer, while greatly desiring superlegato harmonies, may yet write *senza pedale* (without pedal) as a guide to the fingers and as warning against an over-use of the pedal. An illustration of this is to be found in Godard's *En Valsant, Op.* 53, *No.* 6, which in the beginning is marked *molto Ped.* (much pedal), and nine measures later, *senza pedale;* many measures after occur the words *senza pedale il seguente* (the following without pedal). Only a very large hand could accomplish the desired connection of tone without resorting to the pedal. A person with a small hand would be obliged to forego the purity of tone gained by lack of pedal and would be forced to use the pedal a little to sustain and connect tone, despite the composer's express prohibition in the words *senza pedale. Senza pedale* often means without pedal, if this be in accordance with the judgment of the player. Its meaning is elastic, somewhat as is the meaning of the words *senza tempo,* examples of which are to be found in the first movement of Beethoven's *Concerto, in E,* in Schumann's *Allegro, Op.* 8, and in the *Adagio* of Mendelssohn's *Sonata, Op.* 6, in all of which the passages so marked are not without tempo,

but in free tempo, *rubato, con discrezione, quasi improvisazione,* or like a recitative.

Example 142
Schumann — Sonata for Violin and Piano, Op. 121.

Notable instances of sounding rests occur in Schumann's *Sonata for Piano and Violin, Op.* 121. In the sixth measure of the first movement a staccato chord on the first staccato note beat of the measure, written in eighth-notes, sustained is followed by rests in the remainder of the meas-measures of ure and for two succeeding measures, during reats which the violin has a passage in sixteenths. But Schumann also places under this staccato chord the sign *Ped.* ; and the sign & for the release of the pedal does not come until after the middle of the second measure following. This clearly indicates the composer's wish that his written rests should be destroyed by the use of the pedal, so that the chord should continue to sound for nearly three measures, forming a harmonic foundation and background for the violin passage.

A similar instance is found eleven measures after, where a syncopated chord which is attacked on the last beat of the measure and held for one beat in the next should

Acciaccatura bass-note sus-be sustained all through the measure, during the tained through second and third beats; for although the rests are written by Schumann, so also are the signs *Ped.* and , leaving no doubt that these rests are intended for the fingers only and not for the ear. The bass note *Ah,* which Schumann characteristically writes as an acciaccatura-grace, should also sound with the chord, being written as a grace-note because of the impossibility of holding it with the fingers. In such cases it is necessary to strike the important bass-note marcato, and immediately after striking it the pedal should be employed to sustain the tone.

When Schumann employs the sign of the pedal he is extremely careful to indicate exactly his meaning. In the first short staccato two measures of this same sonata the pedal marks with pedal

show that the notes of the staccato chords in these and the three succeeding measures are to be prolonged a little longer than their value as written, but without destroying entirely the effect of rest. The composer further indicates his desire for this effect by the use of the word *kurz* (short) at the same time as the word *Ped.* This is a case in which the pedal is used simultaneously with the fingers instead of afterwards; the object being to strengthen the volume of tone and give the chords an orchestral quality otherwise unobtainable. Both pedal and fingers should be used in a staccato manner, and, as Schumann directs, with energy. The acciaccatura chords from Beethoven's *Sonata, Op.* 57, shown in *Example* 31, should be played in this manner, but with louder, more vigorous orchestral coloring, as should also the C's at the end of each of the two scales introducing the theme in the Solo of the first movement of his *Concerto in C minor.*

This form of pedal technic should be practised by the student until it is easy for him to obtain pedal-staccato, in pianissimo, forte and fortissimo sforzando, and with all qualities of semi-staccato and staccatissimo.

The alternation of pedal effect with fingers and pedal effect with pedal is a form of technic of which the player must continually avail himself if he is to connect and susduced alter-tain tones with purity. And often the use of nateiy by hand fingers without pedal is very necessary. The only andbyfoot 6 .. J -f / way to preserve the pizzicato effect of the staccato notes in measures two and four of the above exercise is to use the pedal as indicated by the rests and notes on the pedal-line. In measures one and three the pedal is used immediately after striking the first chord, so as to sustain it while the right hand plays the accompanying chords; but in measures two and four the use of the pedal is delayed until after the staccato notes are played, so as to preserve the staccato effect of the pizzicato octaves in the left hand.

Example 147
Schubert — Sonata, in Bb major. Andante.

Andante sostenuto *col Pet.*

But notes written staccato are often long-sustained, as is shown in the above example from the slow movement of Schustaccatonote bert's posthumous *Sonata, in B.* In the first coipedaie measure the words *col Ped.* (with pedal) are marked under the staccato bass-note, and the sign for pedal release comes forty-two measures later. This merely means that the bass-notes should be sustained and connected without blurring the melody. The sostenuto pedal could be employed advantageously to do this. Schubert very rarely uses any pedal signs, though we find *mit Verschiebung* in the Trio of the *Sonata, Op.* 42; *pp una corda* in the second movement of the *Sonata, Op.* 53, and ten measures later, *p tutte corde; sordini ppp* many times in the slow movement of the *Sonata, Op.* 143; and *sempre peddle* in the first measure of the song *Sei mir gegrusst* (Angel of Beauty).

Example 148

Schumann l — Albumblatter, Vision, Op. 124, No. 14.

In Schumann's *Albumblatter, Op.* 124, *No.* 14, the piece begins as in the above example, and throughout No indication of its entire length of sixteen measures, all in the Dedal release same general style, no other pedal-mark occurs. There is no mark for pedal release.

Example 149

Schumann — Carnival, Op. 9, No. 9.

if quasiCoeni TM *?f*

Occasionally the instrumentation of a piece is so strongly in the imagination of the composer that he gives some hint of it in the text, as in the above measures from the 0rchestral *Op. 9, No. 9, Papillaris,* where, besides the call coloring sugfor the pedal and the sforzando, the words *quasi* gested m words *Corni* (like horns) serve as an intimation of the musical character, and as in Bach's *Capriccio On the Departure of a Very Dear Brother,* in which two of the movements bear the titles *Air of the Postilion* and *Fugue in Imitation of the Posthorn,* respectively.

Orchestral effect of full, wide-spread, sustained harmonies accompanying a legato melody can be obtained by one hand orchestral effect *sone* if the damper-pedal be correctly employed, produced by one The above study should be played by a single hand hand and pedal &t & **time:** first **with the** ieft hand **alone,** then by the right hand alone. The melody should be well brought out by a proper subordination of the other parts, each of which has its own varied tone-colorings.

Even a single finger, assisted by the pedal, can create fine orchestral effects of melody supported by sustained harmonies orchestral effect of wide compass, as is shown in *Example* 151, produced by one where the second finger of one hand is used to ger and pedal produce the tones which the damper-pedal is employed to hold, in order that the same finger may be free to be removed, to produce, one after another, the melody tones and the notes of the harmonies. The Italian terms in parentheses signify that the melody notes should be *mp,* well marked and held and connected with the pedal; the notes of the accompaniment should be played *pp,* very lightly, and superlegato should be produced by means of the pedal.

Beauty of tone is dependent not only upon the manner of attack and release of the keys but also upon the way in which the damper-pedal is used (its attack, release or Tone sustained partial release, the frequency of its application) by silent re-presand upon the number of pedals used. It is fasci-sure of key nating to observe what a variety of tints maybe obtained in even a single tone after it is produced. Let the pedal sustain a tone while the finger leaves the key; then silently replace the finger on the key and release the pedal; finally, press the pedal frequently, at the same time allowing the keys to rise several times but half-way, only to be again depressed. All this, which takes long to tell, should be rapidly done, and there will be heard a delightful diversity of tone-coloring, the fineness of which depends upon the instrument even more than upon the player.

In a similar manner, though more slowly, by the alternate use of fingers and pedal, purity of melodic outline may be maintained by the performer while playing The sign different harmonies, and the melodic vibrations *t=D* are not only sustained but are also renewed and strengthened each time the pedal frees the strings from the dampers. In the following example the upper staff represents the effect of sustained tone which is obtained. The two lower staves show how this melody in thirds is unbrokenly sustained. Signor Gorno has devised the sign i i as an indication that the hand which has been removed from certain keys should return to them and, with convenient fingers, silently press the keys again, so as to keep the dampers raised from the strings after the pedal pressure is removed, in this way obtaining sustained and unbroken tone by not renewing the attack of the hammer upon the string. Thus the unblurred melody can be played legato, while the accompaniment can be played staccato.

The only way in which such effects can all be obtained in this and in other similar passages (such as are constantly occurring in piano music) is to make use of this silent CZ pressure of finger upon key, in combination with the use of the damper-pedal.

Example 153

Grieg.— In the Spring, Op. 43.

Such a manner of playing is necessary in rendering the closing measures of Grieg's Lyric piece, *In the Spring, Op.* 43, which can be played correctly only by means of silent re-pressure of the fingers upon the octave *B,* which the left hand was obliged to quit in order to play the F# on the highest staff. Grieg's own notation for the left hand consists of the octave *B* written in the customary manner, in dotted-whole-notes; but for the purpose of clearly demonstrating the means by which the bass, melody and inner voices can be connected to those in the succeeding measure without blurring the tones of the dotted-halfnotes D# and Di, the octave in *B* is so written that the silent replacing of the hand upon these keys on the second beat can be indicated by the sign I I The hand should be used in this manner, and the pedal employed twice in the first measure, so as to sustain D# and connect it to *D),* then *D* is connected to C# without blurring any of these tones. In the meanwhile the bass is sustained, for the dampers are kept raised by fingers and pedal alternately. This is the only means of playing so as to interpret correctly Grieg's conception of legato in all the voices and a distinct progression of the tones of the interesting melodic voice, £#, D), *OK.*

Harmonics

The silent pressure of the fingers may be used to effect a charming close to an arpeggio. After the arpeggio is played, and while it is being sustained by the pedal, silently replace the fingers on certain of these keys and then release the pedal, as shown in the third measure of the above example. The chosen tones, corresponding with the keys pressed, will continue to sound while others, released both by pedal and finger, have ceased, and the richness of these sustained tones may be increased by again pressing the pedal as indicated in the fourth measure, on the pedal-line.

When a string is in vibration it produces not only the principal tone heard but also, much more faintly, the intervals of the octave above, the 12th, the 15th, etc. It is the presence of these harmonics, or overtones, which gives to the fundamental tone its fulness. In sustaining tones of an arpeggio in the lower part of the piano it is best to follow, as nearly as possible, this natural sequence of related tones, and to emulate the example of the great pianists, who rarely sustain with the pedal a closed octave deep in the bass, but release the tones filling up the octave before employing the pedal to hold the bass and other tones. Otherwise many dissonant overtones are generated, and the tone, instead of being full and richr sounds thick.

Therefore, in playing these measures from the Mozart *Fantasie, in D minor,* the *F* and the *A* in the left hand should not be sustained beyond their apparent value of an eighth by either fingers or pedal, but the octave *D* should be held by the fingers, and the use of the pedal delayed until after the second *D* is

sounded, so as to sustain, in the left hand, only the open octave.

Some overtones are much fainter than others, but the more sonorous and carefully made the piano, the less the undesirable harmonics are noticeable, and the more distinct Esthetic use of those harmonics which are most useful to the overtones pianist. "You have discovered the secret to lessen to an imperceptible point that unpleasant harmonic of the minor seventh, which has heretofore made itself heard on the eighth or ninth node of the longer strings to such a degree as to render some of the finest chords cacophonic," wrote Berlioz to Steinway. The best harmonics, that is, the octaves and the fifths, in a fine piano are strong enough to be heard distinctly when separated from their fundamentals. Even in the higher registers of the piano any one of these overtones can be obtained and isolated from its fundamental by the silent pressure of a finger upon a key corresponding to its pitch, and sounded by itself without striking the strings corresponding to its pitch.

Until the cause is known it is most astonishing to hear tones to induce which neither the strings nor even Tones appearing the keys have been touched by hammer or by of themselves finger. Hans Schmitt gives an illustration in which overtones, Eolian in their evanescent sweetness, appear of themselves an octave, and a twelfth, above the highest tones directly produced by striking keys.

A delightful effect resultant from sympathetic resonance may be employed by self-accompanied vocalists to get echo A vocalist's effects such as are suitable in pastoral songs, echo effect yodels, etc. By keeping the foot upon the damper pedal, and throwing the voice against the sounding-board of the open piano while singing two or three final tones belonging to the same harmony, a most realistic and sylvan echo will be returned. Beautiful as is this effect, never but once has the writer heard it from the concert stage.

By resorting to this echoing power of the piano a prolonged trill may be made to close with spectral daintiness,

if it is begun with great strength, evenness and brilliancy, and continued at the same speed *dscrescendo,* the player ultimately removing the fingers from the keys, when the piano will for some time continue the trill. The impression upon the hearer will be greater, however, if the fingers simulate playing, as this induces him to listen for the sound more closely than when the hands are removed from the keyboard. The great artists not infrequently employ this method of trilling, decreasing the sound to the finest pianissimo, then gradually working up, *crescendo,* to a climax. A trill can be played in this way with comparative success, even upon a poor piano.

Esthetic trills

But these are not isolated instances of surprising pedal effect; they are only a few of the many equally interesting effects common to the playing of all the great pianists. Scllumann.s In playing the above measures from *The Carnival* notation of overthe chord of nine notes is caused to sound without tones striking their corresponding strings. Many of the tones are but distantly related, and one not at all related, to the preceding sforzato chords, but have been set free in preceding measures by getting the sounding-board and all the strings into strong vibration while keeping the pedal firmly pressed down. By silently depressing the keys of the higher chord, then removing the foot from the pedal, the attacked tones are released, and only the chord of distant music remains. Schumann's own notation of this chord in small notes indicates his desire for this unattacked tone produced by silent pressure of the keys.

Purity of tone is ordinarily desired by the pianist, but there is no musical law which cannot be broken if the poetic feeling calls for it. All the great modern pianists produce dramatic orchestral effects by the use of the pedal in blurring discordant tones, as in the storm of the Wagner-Liszt *Senta's Ballad,* Liszt's *Orage,* the beginning of his *B minor Ballad,* etc. To avoid sullying the tone to an offensive degree, the pedal should be lightly pressed, raised and depressed again, whenever the blurring of tones threatens to grow unpleasant. Often, in order to produce the desired effect, the pedal is kept in constant agitation, in which case it is said to be trilled. The pedal can be used in this manner without releasing the important bass tone and others sonorously played.

Blurring of tones is not allowable save in cases where a well-conceived characteristic tone-coloring can be obtained only by its means. For instance, most pianists play the DescriptiTe last movement of Chopin's *B minor Sonata* with orchestral the pedal down almost continuously, so as to give e ects the right meaning, which Rubinstein interprets thus: "This is a whole drama, with its last movement after the very typical Funeral March, which I would name 'Night winds sweeping over churchyard graves.'"

It is partly by means of blurring the sound that master players express the feeling of Chopin in his *C minor Etude,* which, composed after the fall of his beloved Warsaw, depicts tempestuous passion, destruction, ruin, despair. Cradle-songs, spinning-songs, the murmur of water and the rustle of leaves, — all these can be painted in tones by an esthetic and significant harmonic confusion. Not only do Chopin, Liszt and many other more modern composers abound in such pedal effects; these are numerous in the works of Schubert and Beethoven, and are by no means lacking in the compositions of the great Bach. Such descriptive blurring of tone is very effective if not indulged in to excess, for these indistinct and confused passages act as a foil to the chaste simplicity of pure melodic and harmonic flow, the charm of which in turn is enhanced by the temporarily obscured harmonies. Chopin's *Berceuse,* Liszt's *Spinning Song,* Moszkowski's *In Autumn,* Debussy's *Reflections in the Water,* are pieces which, like thousands of others, contain many passages slightly blurred.

A most peculiar and charming effect occurs twice in the slow movement of Saint-Saens' *Concerto, in F major, Op.* 103. Effect of striking The composer says that the passages in question on glass should sound as though produced by striking upon glass. The effect is caused by use of the pedal in combination with staccato and arpeggiated chords played pianissimo by the right hand, while an altogether different touch is used by the left hand — as is indicated in the notation by the composer's use of both large and small notes.

Music-box effects, so common in the works of Liszt and other modern composers, are produced by delicately playing the keys in the upper part of the piano, while Music-box tones previously elicited sound sonorously, so *eSets* that, with a judicious trilling of the pedal, the dissonances are scarcely heard, as shown in *Example* 158. *(Ped. ten. sino al # signifies pedal held to ».)*

Example 158

Even scales may be played while using the pedal, especially if preceding chords are made to sound distinctly, thus giving a harmonic foundation for the passage, as is shown Scales with by the composer in the following example. The PedaI pedal is pressed firmly down, and, after the chord is struck, is allowed to rise but slightly, and is trilled so as to blot out with the dampers those tones of the passage which are foreign to the harmony of the chord. Such effects occur often in dramatic and descriptive music, and require thoughtful and skilled pedaling. "Above all," wrote Berlioz, "the pianist should know how to use the pedals judiciously." *il Ped.sempn* rami

As, in orchestrating a piece, a composer would not employ to excess the English horn or the oboe, or other instrument of Musicianiy use peculiar coloring, so extremes in pedal effects of the pedals should be used sparingly in order to be relished; one cannot dine on caviar. Purity of melodic line as well as diversity of color is the aim of the musician-pianist, and the pedals should be used with taste, the ear being arbiter of effects. The use of the pedal is largely dependent upon the way in which the fingers are used,— how they produce, sustain and end the tone, and which tones of the harmonies are made most prominent. The pitch of the tones and the rate of speed at which they are played are likewise powerful elements in determining how, when and when not to use the pedal — for occasionally the disuse of the pedal makes a profound impression upon the emotions of the auditor. These many factors in correct pedal usage are some of the causes that contribute to make the pedaling of each artist different from that of his peer; for what would be a correct, even an artistic use of the pedals by one player might be incorrect and bad-sounding if adopted without change by one who used his fingers in some other way.

The conscientious musician rarely uses any means of artistic effect for mere display of virtuosity. We have in this respect a model in the great Russian master whose technical skill was infinite, yet who truly go said: "I play as a musician, not as a virtuoso." The best use of pedal and fingers is that which most completely expresses the conception of the composer; and how difficult of achievement this often is! Verily Chopin's speech was golden when he said: "The correct employment of the pedal is a study for life." /.

CHAPTER XIII

A Word On Technic

Musical understanding comes only with the playing of much music. As the mastering of one composition helps in learning another, there should be a certain finish to the playing of some of the compositions studied, so that the next piece of the same style may get the benefit of previous practice; thus, if the pupil study with the teacher a Beethoven sonata, he should also by himself study one, getting all he can out of it. As Schumann says, he should make *The Well-tempered Clavichord* his daily bread; not only for enjoyment and for the musicianly development which Bach-study brings, but also in order to gain pianistic accuracy,— that distinctness of articulation and clearness of utterance which can be acquired in no other way. In Bach-playing, control is of the first importance, and this form of technic is more difficult to acquire than the technic demanded in Liszt-playing, where flexibility is the main requisite. Daily sight-reading is an essential part of a musician's training, and ensemble playing is necessary for many reasons, one of the most important being the development of a correct understanding of works orchestrally conceived by the composer. The use of a metronome with certain passages helps to a good sense of measure, but this mechanical aid should never be employed throughout a whole work. The true feeling for rhythm and for subtle rubato can be learned only by listening to the performance of such interpreters as Nikisch, Isaye, De Pachmann, Paderewski and Wullner. The singing of lyric songs should not be neglected by the pianist, for this fosters an appreciative love of melody and vocal tone-coloring; nor should the study of operatic scores be omitted, for they cultivate dramatic conception and a good declamation.

The learner should practise studies, many and much, especially those of Cramer, who might be called the Bach of technic; and, for the acquisition of flexibility, Czerny. But it is not practice so much as it is thought that is necessary. The student should ask himself the en prac,ce reason for everything and investigate the causes of his difficulty, which are oftener mental than physical. One can practise technic mentally without touching the piano. It was thus that Billow memorized, in an afternoon, the *Chromatic Fantasie*. A quarter of an hour of practice intently and thoughtfully employed is better than many hours of meaningless or careless practice. What a pity it is that so much wasted effort is given to exercises! Clementi, Cramer, even Chopin and Liszt, do no good with their studies unless the student thinks. What quantities of studies, good in themselves, are put to no purpose and worse by misdirected energy!

If the student were to study other pieces as carefully technically as he studies formal etudes, special technical work would not be necessary. Rosenthal, whose technic is ...... 1,1 Material for perfection, practises in this way; he says there is technical pracno need of special exercises, but that every piece Uce to be found in pieces should furnish material for technical study. This is true

if the mind can be brought to consider the technical requirements of each piece, but it is very difficult for the student to practise interesting compositions mechanically, because there are in these so many things to be enjoyed musically. Schumann recommends the player to devise exercises for himself. Any study may be adapted with reference to special needs by practising it with some of the many possible different fingerings and phrasings, played both legato and staccato, and with various combinations of fingers, hand, forearm and upper arm touches. The position of the hand in pianoforte playing is not, strictly speaking, a natural one. Any one who is asked to lay his fingers on the keys in a natural position will Fundamental incline the hand downward on the side of the little pos"ion of hand finger, and the longer fingers will be stretched out much beyond the shorter ones. But in the cramped position thus caused by depressing the hand on the outside one might practise forever without gaining either strength or skill. It is best to elevate the outside of the hand until the little finger is almost straight, and to contract the second and third fingers, so as to equalize the length of the fingers. Then, if the keys are all struck from the same height above the keyboard and with the same manner of attack, the quality and quantity of tone produced by the fingers will be uniform. In pure finger-touch the knuckles, especially those of the outer fingers, are usually held rather high, and the wrist low, that a touch from the finger alone may be obtained, for it is evident that with a high wrist a pressure from the forearm is unavoidable, as the hand will be depressed when the thumb strikes, and this falling necessitates an involuntary accent. When a low wrist is employed no such falling occurs with the use of the thumb, and the touch from the five equally weighted knuckles results in equality of tonal quantity and quality. It is then easy to add to or to subtract from the weight of any finger, as may be desired. The curved finger touch conduces to brilliancy and facilitates certain kinds of staccato touches.

Flat finger touch, in which the fingers are stretched out almost straight, tends to produce legato, although it may be used also in staccato. This touch is richer and more sympathetic than the curved finger touch. Some of the finest effects result from the fingers remaining in constant contact with the keys, that is, without in the least raising the fingertips from off the keys.

In cases where the thumb is not required to pass under the fingers nor the fingers to pass over the thumb much ease as well as accuracy in playing will be gained by

Position of hand...,.,,,,, favoring the 4th turning the wrists inward, towards the center of and the sth tne keyboard, with the fingers pointing towards the ends of the keyboard, so that the hands are inclined at an angle to the keyboard, thus:

Left Hand. Right Hand.

The better position gained for all five fingers by this outward inclination of the hand is one reason why it is desirable to hold the fourth and the fifth fingers close together, even at times striking with both fingers together on one key. Besides, this way of playing, as well as the use of the third, the fourth and the fifth fingers simultaneously on one key, gives strength and a sonorous quality of tone. The use of the third finger in chords where the fourth and the fifth fingers are employed on different keys, puts "the hand out of position; therefore, when it can be used, the second finger is preferable in connection with the fourth or the fifth finger.

But in playing scales, arpeggios and other combinations of notes in which the main difficulty lies not in the management of the fourth and the fifth finger but of the thumb, Position of *hand* the problem is different. It is obviously impossible favoring the to turn the thumb under and at the same time thumb to incline the hand outward or even to keep it parallel with the keys, and a little experimenting will convince the player that if the hand be turned somewhat inward, with the fingers pointing toward the center of the keyboard — the reverse of the former position — the thumb will pass under with greater ease than in any other position, and without altering its angle of inclination, in playing a scale. With equally weighted and controlled knuckles and a glide of the arm smooth passages will result, provided that while playing the inner ear vividly hears an ideal scale while the fingers reproduce it. As is the case in all technic, velocity is largely a mental quality. When speeding a ball in golf or tennis the mind is fastened mainly upon the point aimed at and not upon the point of attack, and similarly in playing a wide skip or a long scale the mind swiftly should be aimed at the ultimate tone. Since it takes a fraction of a second to depress the keys, this mental tone very slightly and imperatively precedes as well as accompanies its reproduction in piano-tone. When the inner hearing of ideal tones is carried very swiftly toward the ultimate tone, so swiftly as almost to ignore the starting-point and intermediate tones (yet at the same time with a sub-consciousness of them), then the music will be reproduced on the piano with a like speed, providing that there is flexibility of joint and elastic strength of muscle. Without this instantaneous and expressive mental pre-hearing and dictation a fine musical rendering is impossible, no matter how much training in mechanism the fingers, hand and arm may have received. When a sharp staccato is desired the mental tones must be of a precise shortness. When the tones should be songful and long-sustained the accompanying mental melody must be full, continuous and flowing. The difference between players principally depends upon the intensity of the hearing of the imagination. Providing the technic is adequate, the conception, be it noble or trivial, is instantaneously mirrored in the responsive interpretation.

While it is to Bach that we owe the establishment of the most common formula of scale fingering and a methodical and intelligent use of the thumb in turning it under jngtnng the fingers, for Qe wag j.Qe grg. musician 0f high standing who recommended that the thumb be used to perform its natural function in scale playing, instead of allowing it to hang down, cumbrously and uselessly,— it is to Chopin, and after him to Liszt and to von Billow, that we owe a scientific elaboration of this branch of technic. Chopin often advocated the turning of the thumb under the little finger when either cantabile playing or speed was to be gained by this means. Such a manner of playing implied an inclination of the hand even greater than that adapted to the usual fingering, so that the thumb could be prepared thoroughly over the key next to be struck by it. This was not his only innovation; he frequently used his thumb upon the black keys. With what horror did those of the old school look upon this new form of technic! What must Czerny have thought of this style of fingering? — Czerny, who in his *Letters to a Young Lady* writes: "As to what must be observed or avoided in any regular system of fingering: First; when several keys are to be played, one after another, either in ascending or descending, and five fingers are not sufficient for the purpose, the four longer fingers must never be turned over one another; but we must either pass the thumb under, or pass the three middle fingers over the thumb. Secondly; the thumb must never be placed on the black keys. Thirdly; we must not strike two or more keys with the selfsame finger." As to Czerny's remark about the longer fingers being turned one over another, we well know that the playing of thirds and sixths as well as a cantabile style in general has been made much easier by the frequent violation of this rule — a violation so common as to have become, not merely the exception which proves the rule, but a law in itself and one of infinite value. Legato in the outer parts frequently can be obtained only by this means, which, thanks to the boldness of Chopin, is now taught as a part of the technical equipment of the student. As to producing two or more consecutive tones by means of the same finger, we now do this perforce in almost every piano composition; besides which, the player often prefers such fingering as a means of obtaining a certain quality of tone different from that gained by using successive fingers. These things Chopin taught, by example, by precept, and by the fingering which he sometimes marked in his own compositions.

We often hear it said of this or that person that he has a beautiful touch. It might be more correct, perhaps, to say touches, as the myriad of tone colors of which a .,,. 11. -i i it Many touches pianist avails himself is primarily dependent upon the diversity of his technical equipment, although with an artist mechanical skill is only supplementary to the higher attributes of an emotional and intellectual comprehension of the work he interprets; for technic has no intrinsic value, and is to be cultivated as a means, not as an end in itself.

Those touches should first be mastered which are most used. These touches are: finger-legato and finger-staccato, martellato-legato and martellato-staccato. The first of these to be studied and the most difficult to acquire is pure fingertouch, pianissimo. This is of the greatest possible value though it is but little taught. Indeed, it is a difficult thing to get pupils to practise; beginners, especially, cannot perceive the use of playing softly, and it is wasted time to try to persuade them to it. Even advanced students do not practise it much; yet it is of infinite value, as by means of soft playing with the unaided finger flexibility and accuracy of touch are gained, and the finger acquires great sensitiveness and the ability to produce variety of tone color. In practising this touch all of the fingers should rest easily upon the keys except the one which is in the act of striking; this should be raised without stiffness from the knuckle and should descend without assistance from the strength of hand or wrist, and without strain, almost as though falling of its own weight. The wrist should be low, so as to permit of this touch from the knuckle alone. As Thalberg expresses it, the hand should seem boneless. The fourth and the fifth fingers are naturally weak and the thumb is clumsy, yet free and even action of each of the five fingers should be acquired, and except when variety is desired, there should be no difference in the quality of the tones produced by them.

After acquiring a legato touch and perfect evenness of stroke, let tone color be considered in the playing of all scales, arpeggios, exercises and etudes. On the organ cga o ouc and on the stringed instruments a prolonged tone can be sustained unchanged in quality and be connected to another tone; not so on the pianoforte, where only a makeshift legato can be obtained. As no two pianofortes are exactly alike in their mechanism, so, in the attaining of legato, the touch must necessarily vary somewhat with the instrument played. Mere connection of tone, alone, will not produce legato, which is attained not only by the connection of tone but by the avoidance of an effect of attacked tone, which is in opposition to slurred legato — cantabile. A succession of connected tones may be produced on the pianoforte with such an attack of each tone that the tones sound staccato. The reverse also is true: connected tones may be played in such a manner that they sound staccato. Legato should be practised with staccatotouch and stacca-to with legato-touch, as well as in the usual way.

Several of our most noted pianists produce some of their effects through this legato produced with staccato-touch (to coin a new expression). Rosenthal plays with a staccato-touch supplemented with the pedal, iegato effect and by this means gains distinctness of articula-with staccatotion and brilliancy, and the organist Guilmant often used a staccato touch for clarity in lega-to passages. In all pianoforte playing the attainment or failure of an effect should be judged, not by the appearance of notes, fingers and keys, but by the audible result of their use. Legato tones are legato only when they sound legato, and the pianist should cultivate, above all else, an acute, critical and hearing ear.

Practical conditions also aid in determining the manner of execution. The degree of sonority and of mechanical perfection in the instrument used and the size unmusical and acoustics of the

concert hall necessarily must conditions be' taken into consideration in public performance. Many things extraneous to the' composition may influence the touch. For instance, an organist playing on the great organ at Music Hall, in Cincinnati, finds it desirable, on account of the immense distance of the instrument from the audience, to play all legato passages with staccato touch, in order that they should sound legato. Legato-playing, true, unattacked connection of tone, as the organist would hear it, would result in blurred tone, as heard by the audience. To cite another case: the organist accompanying the May Festival Chorus in this hall invariably has to face the unpleasant and the unmusical fact that in order to make a good ensemble with the choral and orchestral bodies, which are situated much nearer than he to the audience, he is obliged to play about a beat ahead of what he hears. He is compelled to violate his own sense of hearing, and to anticipate, in his playing, the conductor's beat as seen in the mirror, and is guided as to the ensemble by his experience as gained at rehearsals; otherwise the audience would hear the organ tones approximately a beat after they heard the same notes sung by the other instruments and by the voices. These, of course, are exceptional and extreme cases of playing in one way in order that the music may sound, not as the player hears it, but as he desires his auditors to hear it.

Finger-staccato and finger-legato are two different ways of using the same touch; the attack is the same, the difference staccato vs. lying wholly in the manner of ending the tone, legato There are many grades of staccato, varying from a slight detachment of the tones, where the unwritten rests (called for by the staccato marks) are short, to a very crisp, sharp staccato, where the rests between the tones are longer, and the tones themselves are of short duration. The old Stuttgart school is largely responsible for the erroneous idea that staccato notes should always be played from the wrist. Both staccato and legato may be produced in any way desired —

from finger, wrist or arm, finger-touch being by far the most frequently needed.

The *martellato* touches, both staccato and legato, consist of rather loud, hammered, and somewhat brassy tone, produced Martellato by the fingers reinforced by the strength of the touches hand. There should, at first, be no movement of wrist or arm. From these four touches come an infinite variety, shading from *ppp* to *ff* and from a very short staccato to the most sustained legato.

To get rich, sonorous tones such as are employed in playing cantabile, play the keys with the fleshy part of the fingers and cantabiie: g deep into the keys with weight from the arm touch forearm and often from the shoulder, so as to induce the full vibrations of the strings. It is best not to play from a height but from near the keys. This cantabile touch is superior to those in which arm touch is omitted, and cannot be imitated by any self-playing mechanism except the Welte-Mignon piano. It is recommended by Beethoven, who said: "Place the hands over the keyboard in such a position that the fingers need not be raised more than is necessary. This is the only method by which the player can learn to *generate* tone and, as it were, to make the instrument sing."

These fundamental positions are, however, by no means the only ones which the hand and fingers may take. Modern pianists employ the arm very largely in Thumb on tip. combination with these touches. In fact, some standing hand pianists use arm weight continually. However, the touch and the position to be assumed are determined by the musical and technical demands of the passage, and the best means to secure the effect desired should be chosen. When the thumb is used alternately on white and on black keys it is often well to play with an undulating wrist, which should be held low when playing on the white keys and raised high when a black key is to be used. A good illustration of this manner of playing is to be found in the left-hand part of Chopin's *F minor Etude, Op.* 10.

Example 160

The middle *C* may be played by the thumb lying in normal position, on its side, the wrist dropped low; and the *D* may be struck with the point of the thumb while the wrist is elevated. Even a standing hand may often be employed to advantage, as in glissando, where the player breaks the continuity of the run just before the final tone, in order to give it melodic force, and strikes the key with the tip of the finger, the wrist raised high above the keyboard.

In legato playing all effort at tone production should cease the instant that the tone is sustained, and the muscles should feel elastic and the joints loose. The wasted greater the feeling of ease in tone production the efiort more control has the player of quality and quantity of tone. With complete relaxation combined with properly directed weight great volume of tone can be produced with almost no effort. Examination of and experiment with a model pianoaction such as pictured on page 160 convincingly proves that when in producing tone a key is put down to its lowest depth, additional pressure exerted against it produces no movement of any part of the action or of the string, and consequently that no alteration in tonal quality and no addition to tonal quantity ensues (although, as shown in the preceding chapter, much can be done to alter the tone by judicious manipulation of the rising and falling key and of the pedals, so as to control harmonics by means of the dampers, while preventing the hammer from re-attacking the string).

A main technical requisite is that there shall be no stiffness of any joint, neither of knuckle, wrist, elbow, shoulder, nor Rigidity. neck. Then the muscles are necessarily elastic.

Affectation A loose wrist is most easily obtained by thinking of the shoulder and elbow joints and seeing that they are flexible, in which case the wrist automatically becomes flexible; while a too concentrated attention upon the wrist itself often actually produces stiffness instead of flexibility. (A somewhat similar psychological condition affects the automobilist, who, for the first time guiding his machine, finds it necessary in order to avoid collision with an approaching team to cease his desperate attempts at avoidance, and to direct his attention to some other object.) Especially should the thumb feel easy in the joints and be flexible in movement. It should experience no sense of strain or of effort. A rigid thumb is often the cause of a stumbling performance, for a continuous physical rigidity produces mental immobility and anxiety and not only prevents the expression of musical feeling but even strangles the feeling itself. When a player of emotional gift plays with undue muscular tension, expending more strength than is needed (and this often occurs, especially in cantabile passages, when he vainly tries to press out more tone after the full tone already has been elicited), the subsequent relaxation, necessary in order to be able to produce beautiful tones, often is accompanied by obtrusive rotary movements of wrist, elbow and shoulder joints, and by awkward motions of the head and even of the whole body, mannerisms which usually are attributed incorrectly to "affectation." These movements are merely strenuous efforts at relaxation while at the same time maintaining the tension. Unnecessary muscular pressure also tends to pinch and to harden the quality of tone and to make impossible a large sonority.

Although there should not be a vain effort to press out additional tone when the tone has already been produced, yet there are both musical and mechanical reasons After-pressure why the fingers should not be completely relaxed 'key after each tone or each short passage. Unrelated single tones and articular subdivisions have no meaning, and even isolated subdivisions have but little meaning in themselves, though these are enjoyed in their relation to the entire phrase, which is heard moving onward to a more complete expression in succeeding phrases as well as in its relation to the composition as a whole. Responsively, the muscular pressure of the fingers and the weight of the hand and arm naturally adjust themselves to the prevailing fluent tension of the phrase, and a certain desirable amount of elastic after-pressure ensues. Mechanically necessary, also, is a certain amount of pressure or weight of the finger on the key, in order to make a sufficiently firm point of departure from which the next playing finger may obtain support. As a rule, only the gifted student overdoes the matter of key pressure; his imagination makes him hear vividly that which he presses the key to obtain, namely, clearly defined and rich crescendo of the tones. The prosaic, unmusical student does not consult his imagination. Piano-tone is what he hears and all he strives for, and his study of tone-color is modeled exclusively after tone he has produced and is producing, and never after ideal tone conceived within himself. With experience, the talented player will overcome his technical fault, but the matter-of-fact pianist can never become an artist.

All the force of pressure should be felt on the key, which bears the entire weight of the stroke from the fleshy part of the finger-tip, in which there should be a conscious sense of weight, of intelligent firmness and easy power, sensitively delicate or generously large, corresponding with the quantity of tone Bending in of needed. Undesirable bending in of a joint, most omts frequently of the nail-joint, is caused by permitting some of the force to waste itself in the joint. With the proper placing of the full weight on the key, this trouble vanishes.

Although the words "pressure" and "weight" are used interchangeably by musicians, in some respects "weight" is Pressure. the preferable term, because "pressure" is apt

Weight 0 *Y,e* mistaken by pupils as meaning excessive additional pressure on the key after producing tone, rather than in its true meaning of tone-producing pressure.

A fault much more common than undue key-pressure, and often combined with it, is that of unconsciously employing Tone produced by simultaneously two opposed forces, namely, force downward motion wlici1 produces tone and force which prevents tone production. Since it is necessary for the fingers to rise sufficiently to permit tone to cease, as well as in order that they may be able to descend on the key from varying heights proportionate to the desired force of the stroke, it is important that raising of the fingers be practised and taught. Tone is produced exclusively by downward motions of the fingers, or of the fingers with added hand and arm weight. When fingertouch is employed, the fingers usually should be raised swiftly and lightly and should instantly descend with vigor, the two movements merging insensibly into one. Analogous to this is the rise and fall of the arm in tacking down a carpet. The arm goes up with elastic ease and comes down forcefully. The upward movement being merely accessory to the downward expenditure of energy, all the thought is given to pounding down the track, and none to raising the arm. Similarly, in producing tone the thought should be of making the key speak by putting it down, not of raising the finger, for, though necessary, this motion does not produce tone. The feeling should be wholly one of muscular energy expended in downward motion.

In piano-playing, all motion of the fingers, hand and arm either is downward motion producing tone, or is preparatory to downward motion. Hence the expressions, "prepare the thumb," "prepare the fingers." Preparation may be made by raising the fingers above the keys or by carrying them laterally across the keys. All preparation should be made quickly, easily, lightly and confidently, and always with the mind concentrated upon the desired tone and the immediate act of striking the key, then the tone-producing downward movements will be full of vigor and without strain. The muscles which move the fingers down and up are in opposed pairs. Those which make the fingers go down are called flexors, and are on the under side of the forearm. Those which raise the fingers are called extensors, and are on the upper side of the forearm. These muscles are connected with the fingers by means of tendons. The finger should not employ simulta-

neously both flexor and extensor muscles, since these then work in opposition and stiffness is the result. In such case the greater the force exerted by the extensor muscle, the harder the opposed flexor will have to work, first to resist the force of the extensor with an equal force, and then to supply sufficient additional force to lower the key and produce tone of the required volume. When the flexor is used without interference from the opposed extensor, this being passive, the finger moves with promptness, easily, and entirely without stiffness, with tonal volume in proportion to the downward expenditure of energy. Of course, stiffness is caused also by excessive and unnecessarily prolonged use of flexor force, as in undue key pressure, for then the extensors have to work too hard to raise the fingers. The shoulder and arm, which, like the fingers, are supplied with muscles of opposed function, should be carefully watched so as to avoid stiffness or tension of these parts, since upon the freedom of all the muscles of the entire playing apparatus depends the ease of playing, and where there is the slightest lack of physical ease the musical feeling will be impaired. The shoulder muscles should never be stiffened, nor should the shoulder be pushed forward and upward, as often happens, nor should the hand or arm be held rigidly quiet.

When the extensors are employed at the same time as their opposed flexors, a great and unnecessary burden is placed upon the flexors. Students often raise their fingers to an extreme height and with such uncompromising force that the opposing muscles which pull the fingers down can barely muster enough force to make the fingers reach the keys, thus causing uncertainty of attack, uneven tone, and stammering performance. Not among the least of the evils following in the train of this habit of stiffening are the pupil's consequent discouragement and lack of self-confidence, for stiffness prevents him from hearing well, and gives him physical discomfort besides. Often lamed hands and arms result from opposing the muscles and then trying to gain strength and

to increase the volume of tone. It is a common fault for players to miss notes because the flexors cannot overcome the powerful upward strain of the extensors, and so they lack strength to depress the keys and sometimes cannot even reach down to them. Sometimes the stiffly moving fingers leave the keys and mount slightly into the air, vainly striving to reach the keys while expending a greater amount of muscular energy in upward motion than in downward motion. Even in public recitals by professed artists we sometimes find it difficult to hear all the notes of a passage intended to be sonorous and brilliant, the performer mistakenly supposing that the harder he works the larger the tone will be, when, in fact, the contrary is the case. Sonorous tone is produced only when there is a dominant feeling of ease and power combined with intense inner hearing of such tone, and with a fervent need of hearing it outwardly expressed. Never should the directing inner conceptional hearing waver or falter for even the fraction of a second, for at the instant of such lapse, and in proportion to the completeness of the lapse, the performance becomes shallow and uninteresting, feeling is reduced to artificial expression, the flow of the cantabile vanishes, soft tone is converted to feeble and uncertain utterance, sonorous tone is transmuted to noisy loudness, passage-work becomes rough and uneven, speed slackens, and self-consciousness takes the place of inspiration.

Every position of the hand and fingers, and all touches, whether of muscle or of weight, which facilitate musianly playing, are good. The mind should be receptive, Rubinstein's so that the player may carefully weigh the first-touch possible advantages of any mode of playing which is new to him. In order to bring out the orchestral coloring demanded by a composition Rubinstein on one occasion even struck an octave in the bass with both fists — but then he was Rubinstein!

The sage proverb, "Practice makes perfect," applies to every art, and especially in music is technical virtuosity demanded. Emerson finely expresses this thought: "The friction in nature is so enormous that we cannot spare any power. It is not question to express thought, to elect our way, but to overcome resistances of the medium and material in everything we do. Hence the use of drill, and the worthlessness of amateurs to cope with practitioners. Six hours every day at the piano, only to give facility of touch; six hours a day at painting, only to give command of the odious material, oil, ochres, and brushes. The masters say, that they know a master in music, only by seeing the pose of the hands on the keys;—so difficult and vital an act is the command of the instrument."

"I have to be diligent," said John Sebastian Bach.

INDEX

C. A series of Educational Text-books suited to the requirements of the average student and covering every essential branch of musical instruction. Uniformly bound in cloth.

PIANO HALF HOUR LESSONS IN MUSIC Mrs. Herman Kotzschmar $1.00
Class work for beginners combining study with play. A practical course for teachers and mothers. Fully illustrated.

BURROWES' PIANO PRIMER Frederic Field Bullard, Editor.50
The rudiments of music with tables of keys, scales, intervals, chords, turns, terms, and a guide to practice.

NATURAL LAWS IN PIANO TECHNIC Mary Wood Chase 1.25
This work presents clearly and concisely the essential laws of the building up of a good
Piano Technic in a practical manner. Fully illustrated.

THE INTERPRETATION OF PIANO MUSIC Mary Venable 1.25
Studios in the meaning of printed signs used in music, and their bearing on the interpretation of standard works. With numerous music illustrations.

PIANO TEACHING: ITS PRINCIPLES AND PROBLEMS Clarence G. Hamilton, A.M. 1.25
A practical book written by a practical man to meet practical needs. Illustrated.

VOICE

A B C OF MUSIC Auguste Mathieu Panseron (Ed. by N. Clifford Page) 1.00
This book is a primer of vocalization, not a complete course in singing. It gives the begin-. ner all the facts which should be mastered at the start,— the A B C's.

TWELVE LESSONS IN THE FUNDAMEN- TALS OF VOICE PRODUCTION Arthur L. Manchester 1.00
Presents in a succinct, clearly stated form the fundamental principles of tone production illustrated by simple, practical exercises.

TRAINING OF BOYS' VOICES Claude Ellsworth Johnson.75
A practical guide to the correct " placing" and training of boys' voices.

RESONANCE IN SINGING AND SPEAKING Dr. Thomas Fillebrown 1.25
A scientific exposition of fundamentals, with breathing and vocal exercises and illustrations. Emphasizes psychology rather than physiology.

COMMONPLACES OF VOCAL ART Louis Arthur Russell 1.00
The plain truths of vocal art presented in simple, untechnical language.

ENGLISH DICTION FOR SINGERS AND SPEAKERS Louis Arthur Russell 1.00
For all singers or speakers who seek a refined or artistic use of the English language. A study of the correct "sounding" of words.

FRENCH DICTION FOR SINGERS AND SPEAKERS William Harkness Arnold 1. 00
The elements of French pronunciation reduced to a few fundamental principles, readily mastered. Contains twenty-one modern songs, besides poems and prose extracts.

VIOLIN HOW TO STUDY KREUTZER Benjamin Cutter.75
What every violin teacher discusses and illustrates in the lesson room put into book form.

OLIVER DITSON COMPANY, BOSTON

Lightning Source UK Ltd.
Milton Keynes UK
UKOW04f2324100117

291826UK00009B/182/P